WHALES AND NIGHTINGALES

Generously donated by
Wanda Petzschler

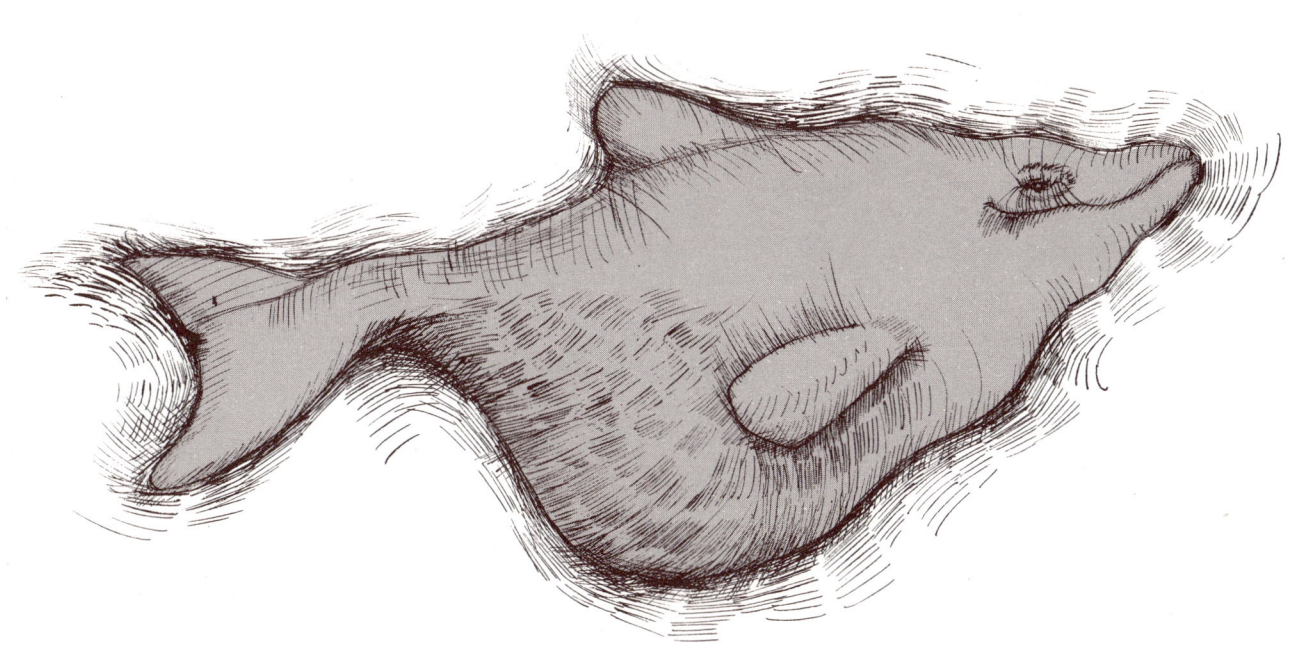

WHALES AND NIGHTINGALES

BASIC GOALS IN MUSIC 4
SECOND EDITION

Earle Terry, B.A., B.Paed., M.Mus.
Director of Music, London Board of Education
Assistant Professor, Faculty of Music
University of Western Ontario

Lloyd H. Slind, B.Mus., L.R.S.M., Ed.D.
Faculty of Education, University of British Columbia

Frank Churchley, B.Mus., L.R.C.T., M.A., Ed.D.
Faculty of Education, University of Victoria

McGRAW-HILL RYERSON LIMITED

Toronto	Montreal	New York	London
Sydney	Johannesburg	Mexico	Panama
Düsseldorf	Kuala Lumpur	New Delhi	Rio de Janeiro

ACKNOWLEDGMENTS

The following songs are reproduced in this book by permission of the copyright owners:

'Simmons, reprinted from *Play Party Book* © 1940 by permission of Cooperative Recreation Service, Inc./The Green Dress, words and music by Josef Marais. Copyright 1943, 1950, 1962 Fideree Music Corporation. Used by permission/Come Let's Dance, words from *Making Music Your Own*, Book 4, © 1968, General Learning Corporation. Reprinted by permission/ Mañana, from *Making Music Your Own*, Book 4, © 1968 General Learning Corporation. Reprinted by permission/An Eskimo Lullaby, English text by Edith Fowke, from *Folk Songs of Canada* by Fowke-Johnston, used by permission of Waterloo Music Company, Ottawa, Canada/The Cricket Takes a Wife, English words by permission of Novello and Company Limited, Sevenoaks, England. Házasodik a tücsok (The Cricket Takes a Wife), Hungarian folk song from the collection *Tizán innen, Dunántúl*. Music used by permission of Ediyio Musica, Zenemükiadó, Budapest, Hungary/Voyageur Song, Copyright Gordon V. Thompson Limited, Toronto, Canada. Used by permission/Spring Round and On the Moor, from *Song of the Country* (Bulman). Reprinted by permission of Granada Publishing Limited, London, England/Haru Ga Kita (Spring Has Come), reprinted from *Sampler of Japanese Songs*, copyright 1958, by permission of Cooperative Recreation Service, Inc./En Roulant, Ma Boule, English text by Edith Fowke, from *Folk Songs of Canada* by Fowke-Johnston. Used by permission of Waterloo Music Company, Ottawa, Canada/Doon the Moor, from *Singing America*: copyright © 1940 by Summy-Birchard Company, Evanston, Illinois. Copyright renewed. All rights reserved. Used by permission/The Little Prince (Le Petit Prince), from *Chantons Un Peu*, translated by Alan Mills, arranger Arthur Morrow. © BMI Canada Limited, Toronto/Land of Cherry Blossoms, by Burton Kurth (words by T. W. Woodhead) from *Sing Hey Ho!* copyright 1951 by Clarke, Irwin & Company Limited. Used by permission/Girl's Dance Song, from *Folk Songs of Europe*. English words by permission of Novello and Company Limited, Sevenoaks, England/The Papaya Tree, Robert W. Winslow and Leon Dallin, *Music Skills for Classroom Teachers*, Dubuque, Iowa: Wm. C. Brown Company Publishers, 1970, p. 161.

Whales and Nightingales
Basic Goals in Music 4
Second Edition

Copyright © McGraw-Hill Ryerson Limited, 1972. All rights reserved. No part of this publication may be reproduced, stored in a retrieval system, or transmitted, in any form, or by any means, electronic, mechanical, photocopying, recording, or otherwise, without the prior written permission of McGraw-Hill Ryerson Limited.
Copyright © McGraw-Hill Company of Canada Limited, 1964.

ISBN 0-07-077456-0

1 2 3 4 5 6 7 8 9   BP 72 10 9 8 7 6 5 4 3 2

Printed and bound in Canada

CONTENTS

		Page
Meet Your Book		x
Syllables and Hand Signs		1
All People That on Earth Do Dwell	Melody from Genevan Psalter, 1551	3
'Simmons (A Party Game)	Southern U.S.A.	4
Lukey's Boat	Newfoundland Song	5
The Deaf Woman's Courtship (A Dialogue Song)	Traditional	6
Rhythm Round		7
The Wishing Well	French Folk Song Freely translated by F. Churchley	8
Reading Music: Time Names		9
Fire's Burning (A Round)	Traditional	10
For Health and Strength (A Round)	Old English	11
My Goose (A Round)	Traditional	11
We're on the Upward Trail	Traditional Camp Song	12
Weggis	Swiss Folk Song	15
Now Thank We All Our God	Johann Cruger Words by Martin Rinckart Translated by Catherine Winkworth	16
The Green Dress	Afrikaans Song	18
King Arthur	English Folk Song	20
Some Folks Do	Words and melody by Stephen Foster	22
Where Is John?	Czechoslovakian Folk Song	23
The Old Woman and the Pedlar	Old English Folk Song	24
The Bell Doth Toll (A Round)	English	25
We Are Musicians	German Folk Song	26
Hallow-e'en	Words and Music by Cyril Mossop	28
Brother, Come and Dance	"Hansel and Gretel", Humperdinck	30
Major Scales		31
Melody		32
There's a Hole in My Bucket	Traditional	34
The Pentatonic Scale		35

		Page
Old Texas (Echo Song)	Oklahoma Cowboy Song	36
A Little Night Music	Mozart	38
The Violin		38
Amsterdam	Music by Mozart Words by Anne Ross	40
Old Joe Clarke	Tennessee Folk Song	42
Who Did Swallow Jonah?	Spiritual (Arr. Earle Terry)	44
Oliver Cromwell	Old English Folk Song	46
Dashing Away with the Smoothing Iron	English Folk Song	48
Rhythm		49
Rig-a-Jig-Jig (Singing Game)		50
Ah! Si Mon Moine Voulait Danser	French-Canadian Folk Song	52
Review 1		54
Bonavist' Harbour	Newfoundland	55
Christmas in Many Lands		56
Deck the Halls	Wales	57
Dance Carol	Sweden	58
Fum Fum Fum	Spanish Dance Carol from Catalonia	59
Echo Carol	Germany	60
Christmas Is Here	Bohemia	61
Patapan	Burgundy Carol	62
My Candles	Song from Israel	63
Michael Finnigin	Traditional	64
Come Let's Dance (A Round)	13th-century France	65
The Greedy Girl	Slovak Folk Song	66
Canoe Song (A Round)	Traditional	68
Syncopation		69
New River Train	American Folk Song	70
Mañana	Spanish Folk Song	71
An Eskimo Lullaby		72
My Hat It Has Three Corners	German Folk Song	73
The Cricket Takes a Wife	Hungarian Folk Song	74
Ifca's Castle	Czech Folk Song	76
Ah! Poor Bird! (A Round)	Traditional	77
Wraggle-Taggle Gypsies, O!	Old English Ballad	78

		Page
The Moldau	Smetana	79
Ach Ja!	German Folk Song	80
Drums and Tambourines	Words by F. Churchley Music by J. Rameau	82
Frère Jacques (A Round)	Traditional	83
Streets of Laredo	American Folk Song	84
Form		85
Review 2		86
Voyageur Song	Words by John Murray Gibbon French-Canadian Folk Song	87
Sweet Nightingale	English Folk Song	88
Slumber Song	Words by Grace Budd Melody by Franz Schubert	89
Heigh Ho, Anybody Home?	English Folk Song	90
Czech Dance		91
Playing the Recorder		92
Harmony		94
Auld Lang Syne	Scottish Folk Song	96
Kookaburra (A Round)	Australia	97
O How Lovely Is the Evening (A Round)	Traditional	98
Edvard Grieg		100
Peer Gynt Suite Theme	Edvard Grieg	101
My Homeland	Words by Joan Field Music by Edvard Grieg	101
Way Up on the Mountain	Savoie Folk Song	102
A la Claire Fontaine	French-Canadian Folk Song	103
Night Herding Song	Cowboy Song	104
Easter Hymn	Cyril Mossup	108
Spring Round	Hungary	109
On the Moor	Iceland	109
Cornish May Song	17th-century English Morris Dance Words by Sir Alexander Boswell	110
Review 3		111

		Page
Who Has Seen the Wind?	Christina Rossetti Music by Earle Terry	112

Haru Ga Kita
    (*Spring Has Come*)
	Japanese Folk Song
	Translation by
	    San-ichi Kesen
		113

Land of the Silver Birch	Ontario Folk Song	114
En Roulant, Ma Boule	French-Canadian Folk Song	116
The Snoring Man	French Folk Song Words by David Warrack	118
Can't You Dance the Polka?	Sea Shanty	120
Doon the Moor	Scottish Folk Song	121
Bonhomme! Bonhomme!	French-Canadian Folk Song	122
Aaron Copland		124
Simple Gifts	Pennsylvania Dutch Folk Song	125
Lullaby	Johannes Brahms	126
Sing Your Way Home	Camp Song	127
All Through the Night	Welsh Air	128
The Little Prince	French Folk Song	129
Santa Lucia	Italian Folk Song	130
Juanita	Spanish Song	131
Charlie Is My Darling	Scottish Folk Song	132
Oh, Dear! What Can the Matter Be?	English Folk Song	133
Land of Cherry Blossoms	Chinese Melody Arr. by Burton Kurth Words by T. W. Woodhead	134
Gin Gang Goo	Traditional	136
Boston Come-All-Ye (*The Fishes*)		138
One of These Days (A Round)	American Folk Song	139
Follow On! (Echo Song)	Old Song	140
Girl's Dance Song	Ukraine	141
Tzena	Israeli Folk Song	142
The Papaya Tree	Filipino Folk Tune	143
Will Ye No Come Back Again?	Scottish Song	144

	Page
Review 4	145
Fingering Chart for the Recorder	146
Glossary of Musical Terms and Signs	146
Index	149

Meet Your Book

This is a new music text book especially written for you.

In this book you will meet many familiar songs but you will also find new rounds, action songs, songs for dramatization, dances, echo songs, poetry written by children of your own age, and special holiday songs.

In some ways this book is really two books in one, because in addition to a fine repertoire of interesting songs it also gives you the opportunity to discover more about sound . . . how to shape sound into melody . . . how to combine melodies into harmony and how to recognize form in music.

You will enjoy playing the simple instrumental accompaniments and creating new melodies and harmonies. If possible, do listen to the recordings suggested throughout the book. It is always interesting to learn how a composer expresses himself through instruments and voices.

Music is exciting. In your imagination it can take you to faraway places and tell you stories of people worshipping, working, and playing. It speaks of the outdoors, of animals and birds, of nature, of your community, of your country, and of your world.

Music helps you to understand life and living, past and present. But most important, it is here today for you to enjoy.

SYLLABLES and HAND SIGNS

A quick, easy way to learn to read music is to use the hand signs and tonic sol-fa syllables shown on this page and in your first six songs.

Each hand sign represents a tone of the scale.

This system was invented in the 11th century and was developed to its present form by an Englishman, John Curwen, in the 19th century.

The tonic sol-fa syllables are:

doh   ray   me   fah   soh   lah   te
(d)   (r)   (m)   (f)   (s)   (l)   (t)

The eighth tone above d is d'; the eighth tone above r is r'; and so on.

The eighth tone below d is d,; the eighth tone below f is f,; and so on.

Each eight-tone series, from d to d', or l, to l, is an octave.

Here is the octave d to d' beginning on the tone C of the bells or piano:

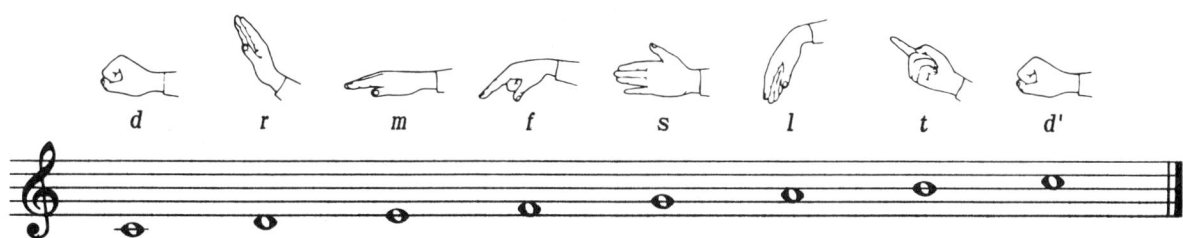

Outdoors

THE TREE TRUNK

The
tree
trunk
shoots
upward,
twists,
bends
and
curves
to
a
point
in
the
sky.

Drew Kirk
Grade Five

THE STREAM

There's a flowing little stream,
Down by the forest,
And that's the place
Where the grass grows best.

There's a laughing little stream,
Down by the forest
And that's the place
Where I like to rest.

Rosemary Burd
Grade Five

INTERVAL PREPARATION

'Simmons

A Party Game

Form a circle, hands joined

Southern U.S.A.

1. Cir - cle left, do oh, do oh, cir - cle left, do oh, do oh,
2. Cir - cle right, do oh, do oh, cir - cle right, do oh, do oh,

Cir - cle left, do oh, do oh, Shake them 'sim - mons down!
Cir - cle right, do oh, do oh, Shake them 'sim - mons down!

Drop hands

Partners, . . . (*Girls on right of boys*.)

3. Balance all, do oh, do oh, . . . (*Dance toward your partner then back to your place.*)

4. 'Round your partners, do oh, do oh, . . . (*Go around your partner, back to back.*)

5. 'Round your corners, do oh, do oh, . . . (*Boys, go around the girl on your left, back to back.*)

6. Prom'nade all, do oh, do oh, . . . (*Dance to your seats.*)

THINGS TO DO

Sing the song to tonic sol-fa syllables, using hand signs.

Clap the rhythm of the beat.

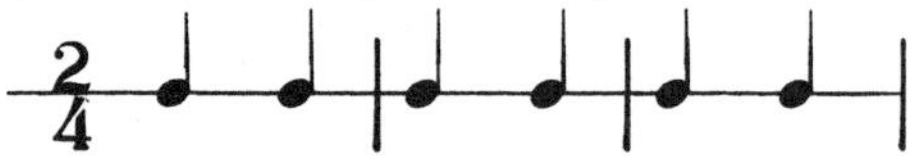

Follow the directions and dance while you sing.
Add a drum for rhythm accompaniment.

INTERVAL PREPARATION

s, d r m r m l, s, d r t, s, r m d s, s, d

Lukey's Boat

Newfoundland Song

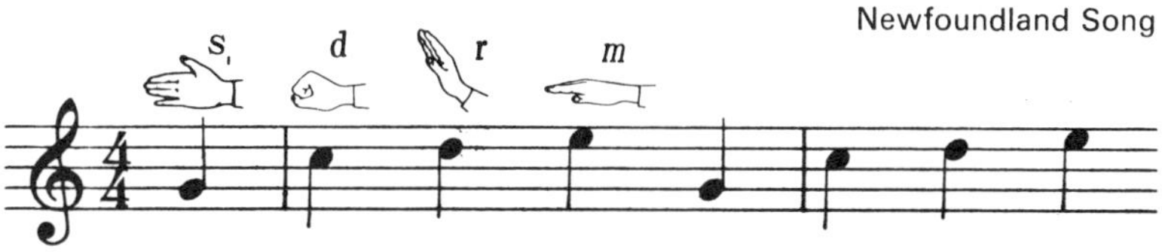

O Lu - key's boat is pain - ted green,
O Lu - key he sailed down the shore,

O Ho   O Ho
O Ho   O Ho

O Lu - key's boat is pain - ted green
O Lu - key he sailed down the shore

It's the fin - est boat you've ev - er seen.
To catch some fish from Lab - ra - dor

O Ho - fol - rid - dle dee dee.
O Ho - fol - rid - dle dee dee.

INTERVAL PREPARATION

The Deaf Woman's Courtship

A Dialogue Song

Traditional

Boys:
1. Old wom-an, old wom-an, Are you fond of cook—-ing?

Girls: Speak a lit-tle loud-er, sir,

I'm ver-y hard of hear—-ing.   hear-ing.

2. Old woman, old woman, Are you fond of sewing?
   Speak a little louder, sir, I'm very hard of hearing.

3. Old woman, old woman, Will you darn my stocking?
   Speak a little louder, sir, I'm very hard of hearing.

4. Old woman, old woman, Will you let me court you?
   Speak a little louder, sir, I just begin to hear you.

5. Old woman, old woman, Don't you want to marry me?
   Oh, my goodness gracious me, I think that now I hear you.

THINGS TO DO

Sing to tonic syllables, using hand signs.
Which tonal patterns are exactly alike?
Create actions to dramatize the text.
Sing verses one to three progressively softer. Suggest tone quality for the old woman and the man.
Suggest dynamic levels for verses four and five.

Conduct two beats to the bar.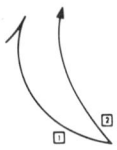

RHYTHM ROUND

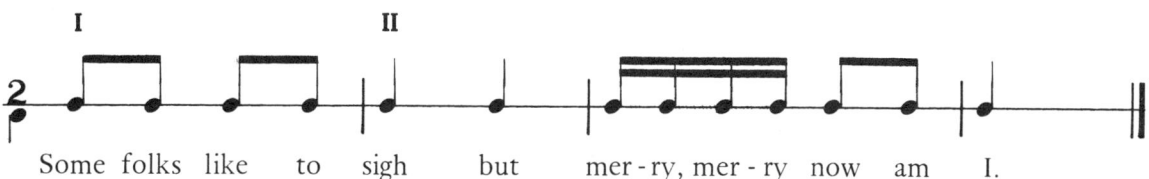

Clap this rhythm.
Chant the words to the rhythm.
When the rhythm pattern is learned, divide the claps into two groups with group 1 slapping the knees to the rhythm. When group 1 reaches bar 2, group 2 starts clapping hands lightly to the pattern.

Repeat the round, group 1 using percussive instruments (drumsticks, etc.), group 2 using melodic instruments (bell, piano, etc.).

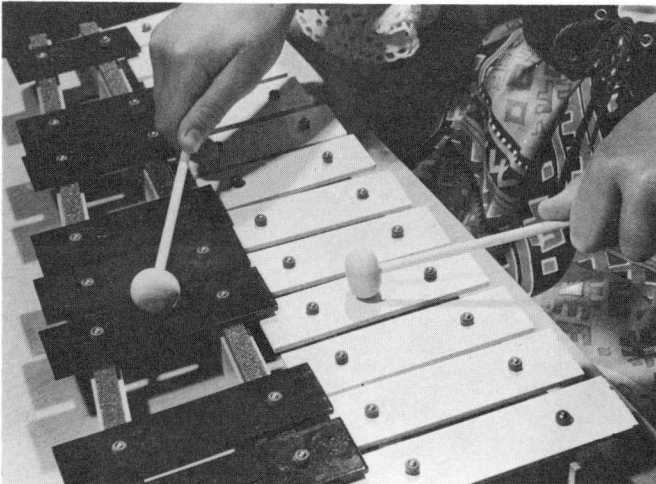

INTERVAL PREPARATION

The Wishing Well

French Folk Song
Freely translated by F. Churchley

Sing to tonic syllables, using hand signs.
Which tonal patterns are exactly alike?

READING MUSIC

TIME NAMES (also called RHYTHM SYLLABLES)

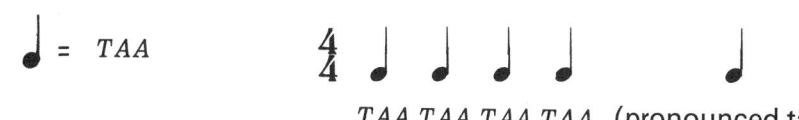

= *TAA*

TAA TAA TAA TAA (pronounced tah)

taa - tai

(pronounced tah-tai)

Read this pattern from "The Deaf Woman's Courtship", page 6.
(Tap or clap the beat of the metre.)

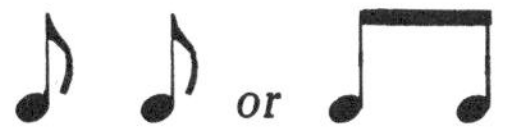

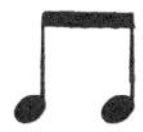

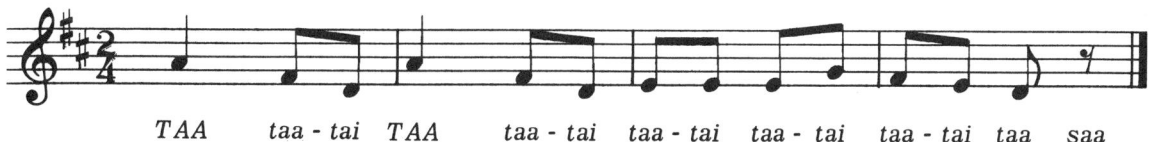

Now turn to the song and read it through to the time names.

Note

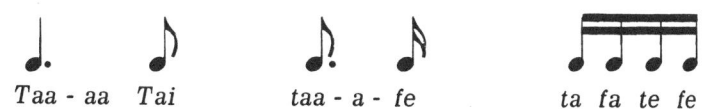

Read this pattern from "Some Folks Do", page 22.

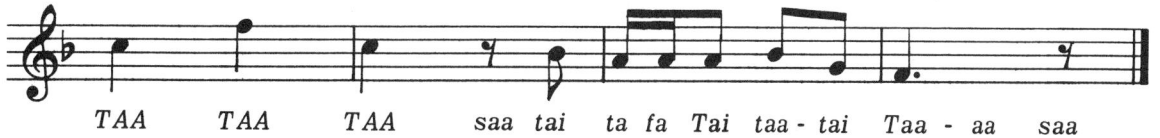

Turn to the song and read it through to the time names.

Read this pattern from "We Are Musicians", page 26.

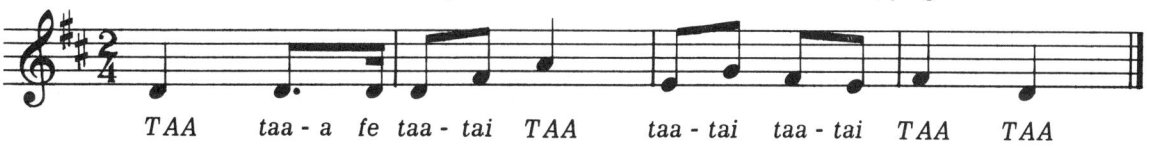

Turn to the song and read it through to the time names.

RHYTHM DRILL

Fire's Burning

A Round

Traditional

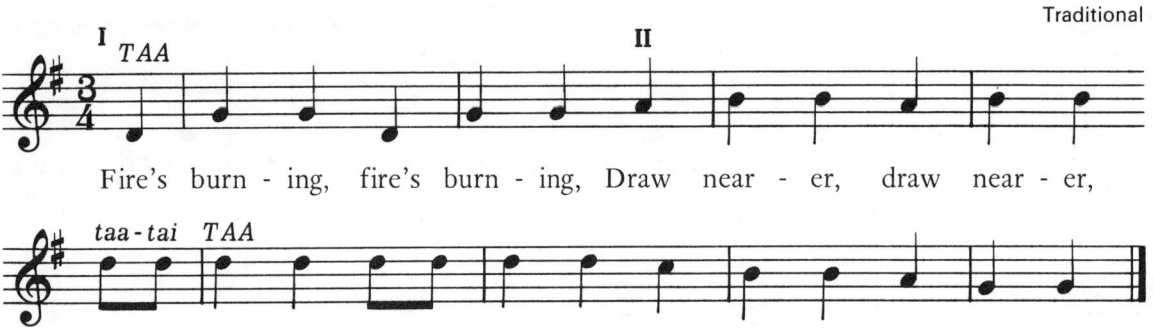

Fire's burn - ing, fire's burn - ing, Draw near - er, draw near - er,
By the camp - fire, by the camp - fire, Come sing and be mer - ry.

THINGS TO DO Sing the time names.
Sing the song through to the tonic sol-fa, using hand signs.
Sing the words. Try the song as a two-part round.

Play soh on the piano or bells as indicated on the staff below.

Sing doh by thinking of the first notes in "Fire's Burning".
Check your pitch by playing doh on the piano or bells.

RHYTHM DRILL

My Goose
A Round

Traditional

Why should-n't my goose Sing as well as your goose,
When I paid for my goose Twice as much as you?

Sing the time names.
Sing the tonic sol-fa syllables, using hand signs.

The three notes that you sang together (d, m, s) are called a *I chord* (one-chord).

For Health and Strength
A Round

Old English

For health and strength and dai-ly food We praise Thy name, O Lord.

11

RHYTHM DRILL

TAA — taa tai — TAA-AA — TAA-AA-AA-AA

We're on the Upward Trail

In march time

Traditional Camp Song

I. TAA taa-tai TAA TAA   II. TAA-AA   SAA SAA

SING: We're on the up-ward trail! We're on the up-ward

PLAY:*

f
TAA-AA

trail!   Sing - ing,   sing - ing,   (Rest!)

f *s* *m*

Ev-'ry-bod-y sing-ing,   As   we   go!

We're on the up-ward trail!   We're on the up-ward

* Left hand only, on the piano.

12

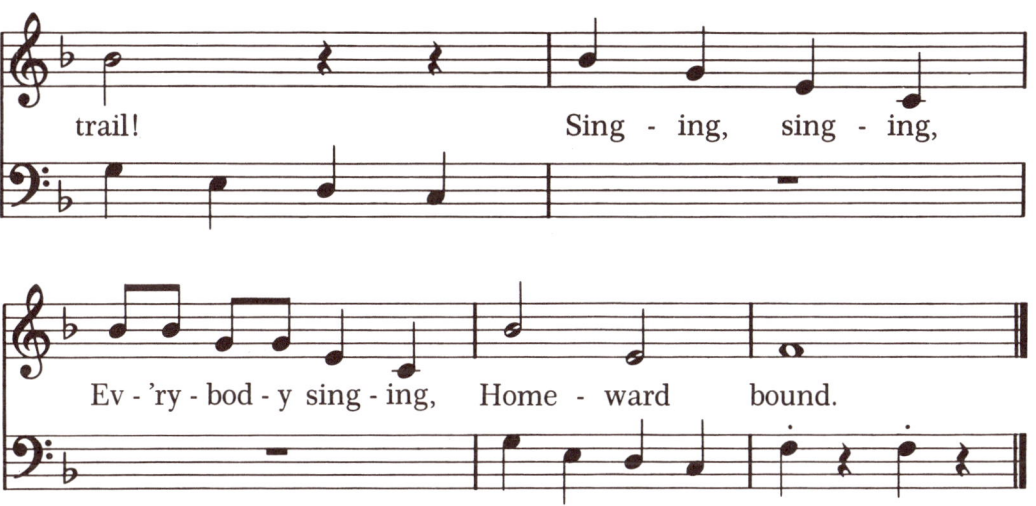

This is a lively camp song. The simple accompaniment may be played by one of you or by the teacher. (Make it sound crisp, with no pedal.) If a piano is not available use bells, or sing the accompaniment an octave higher than it is written.

This song contains examples of quarter notes, eighth notes, half notes, and whole notes. Find them!

Sing the song as a round.

Now sing the song again, using time names. (𝒐 = TAA-AA-AA-AA)

Be sure to sing each note for its proper value, especially the whole notes!

Which bars of the music are exactly the same as the first four bars?

How is the second set of four bars different from the last four?

THINGS TO DO In your notebook, write on the bottom line of the *treble* staff:

1. One bar of eighth notes
2. One bar of quarter notes
3. One bar of half notes

DISCOVER THE SOUNDS AROUND YOU

Listen to the sounds in your classroom, in the school halls, in the school playground, in the street, in the park. Make a list of these sounds.

Listen to the sounds you create using your lips, your mouth, your voice.

Listen to the sounds of snapping, clapping, slapping your knees, tapping.

Listen to the sounds of classroom instruments (soft and loud).

Listen to the recorded sounds of instruments of the orchestra.

Discover which sounds are high or low, loud or soft, long or short.

Discover and discuss which sounds are pleasant and which are unpleasant.

Listen to recorded sounds of nature: "Dance of the Mosquito" by Liadov; "The Flight of the Bumble Bee" by Rimsky-Korsakov; "The Brook" (with bird songs), second movement of Beethoven's Sixth Symphony; "William Tell" Overture (sound of a thunderstorm).

INTERVAL PREPARATION

s, d t, d r r l, r r t, l s t, d d s d

Weggis

Swiss Folk Song

1. From Lu-cerne to Weg-gis on,
2. On the lake we all shall row, Hol-di-ri-di-a, hol-di-ri-a,
3. Weg-gis hills are not so far,

Shoes or stock-ings we won't don,
Look-ing at the fish be-low, Hol-di-ri-di-a, hol-di-a.
We will all shout "Hei-sa-sa,"

CHORUS

Hol - di - ri - di - a, hol - di - ri - di - a, hol - di - ri - a,

Hol - di - ri - di - a, hol - di - ri - di - a, hol - di - a.

Sing the time names.

Sing the tonic sol-fa syllables, using hand signs.

INTERVAL PREPARATION

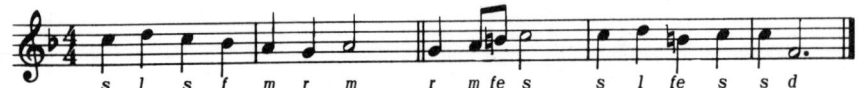

Now Thank We All Our God

Johann Cruger
Words by Martin Rinckart
Translated by Catherine Winkworth

Maestoso

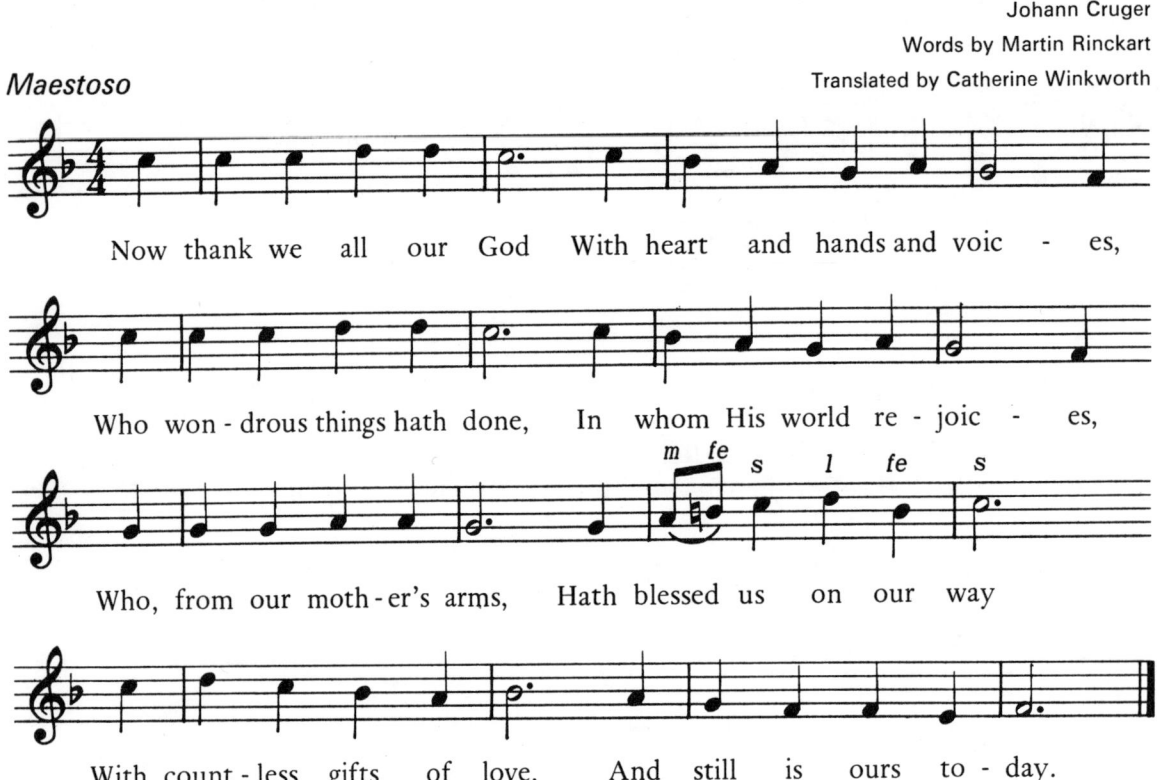

Maestoso means to sing the song in a dignified, majestic style. With only one exception, the melody uses single steps. Find the exception.

INTERVAL PREPARATION

s, d d t, r r r f m r d

The Green Dress

Afrikaans Song

When-ev-er Het-ty has a green dress on, green dress on, green dress on, When-ev-er Het-ty has a green dress on, I will sing a song for her. Let us sing a song, It need-n't be so long, For Het-ty has a green dress on!

Let us sing a song, It need-n't be so long, For Het-ty has a green dress on!

THINGS TO DO   Sing to the tonic syllables, using hand signs.

Clap two beats to the bar. SING THE TIME NAMES

(♩. TAA-AA-AA)

Find phrases which are alike.

> mf means "medium" loud
> p means to sing softly
> ff means to sing loudly (don't shout)

Can you dance the polka? Try it!

On the bells play the notes which go with "green dress on".

Substitute names of your classmates in place of Hetty, and references to blue shirt, yellow ribbon, red tie, brown shoes, etc., in place of green dress.

RHYTHM DRILL

4/4
TAA
taa tai
TAA - aa tai

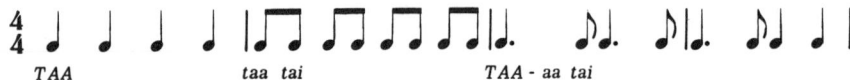

King Arthur

Crisply

English Folk Song

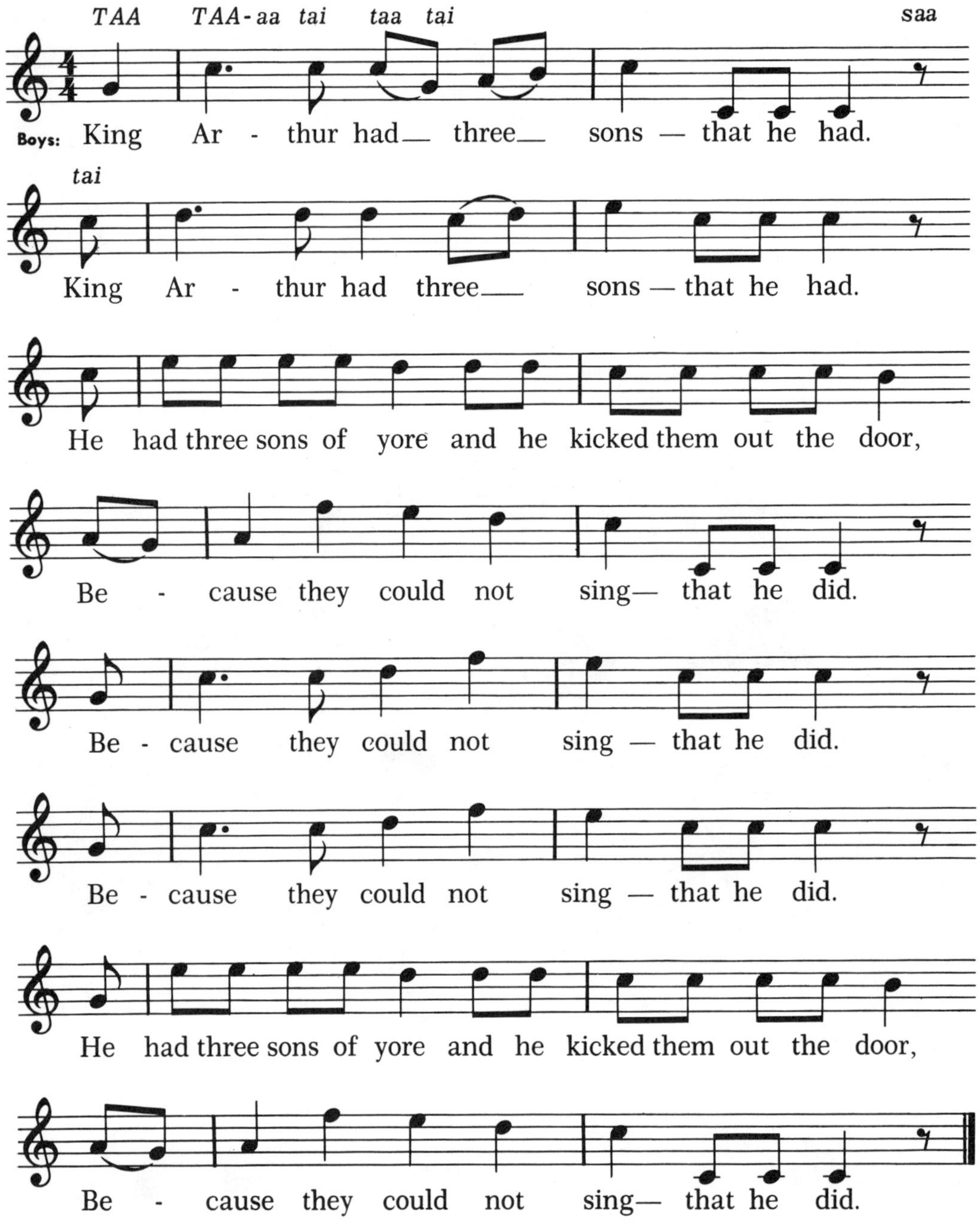
TAA TAA-aa tai taa tai saa
Boys: King Ar - thur had— three— sons — that he had.
tai
King Ar - thur had three— sons — that he had.
He had three sons of yore and he kicked them out the door,
Be - cause they could not sing— that he did.
Be - cause they could not sing — that he did.
Be - cause they could not sing — that he did.
He had three sons of yore and he kicked them out the door,
Be - cause they could not sing— that he did.

Girls: The first he was a miller—that he was.
The second he was a weaver—that he was.
And the third he was a little tailor boy,
And he was mighty wise—that he was.
    And he was mighty wise—that he was.
    And he was mighty wise—that he was.
    And the third he was a little tailor boy,
    And he was mighty wise—that he was.

Boys: Now the miller stole some grain for his mill—that he did.
And the weaver stole some wool for his loom—that he did.
And the little tailor boy, he stole some corduroy,
For to keep those three rogues warm—that he did.
    For to keep etc. . . .

All: Oh the miller he was drowned in his dam—that he was.
And the weaver he was killed at his loom—that he was.
And Old Nick he cut his stick with the little tailor boy,
With the corduroy under his arm—that he did.
    With the corduroy, etc. . . .

THINGS TO DO

The class is divided into two groups. One group sings the solo part while the other group sings the chorus ("That he did", etc.) Notice that you sometimes have to do a little juggling to make the words sound right with the music. (Hint: if you seem to have too many words, sing two syllables under a quarter note, making each sound like an eighth note; if you seem to have too few words, sing one syllable under two eighth notes, making it sound like a quarter note.)

For variety, play the chorus part on the bells, or the piano, or on both instruments. As you play it, sing the names of the time values, "two eighths, quarter". Add percussion instruments (sticks, drum, tone blocks).

Another time, try *not* singing the chorus part, but simply clapping the rhythm ♫ ♩ in its place.

RHYTHM DRILL

TAA　TAA　taa-tai　　taa-a-fe　　ta-fa-te-fe　　TAA　TAA

Some Folks Do

Words and melody by Stephen Foster

Group 1　　　　　　　　　　*Group 2*

Some folks like to sigh,
Some folks fear to smile,
Some folks get grey hairs, } Some folks do,　Some folks do;

Group 1　　　　　　　　　　*Group 2*

Some folks long to die.
Oth-ers laugh through guile,
Brood-ing o'er their cares, } But that's not me nor you.

All sing the chorus

l　　s　m　f　m　r　d　t,　s,　d

Long live the mer-ry, mer-ry heart that laughs by night and day, Like the Queen of Mirth,　no mat-ter what some folks say.

Divide the class into two groups and sing as a dialogue song. Conduct it.

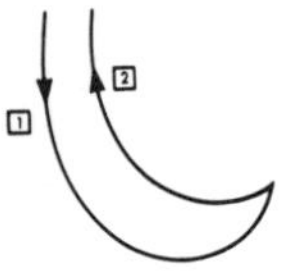

22

RHYTHM DRILL

Where Is John?

Czechoslovakian Folk Song

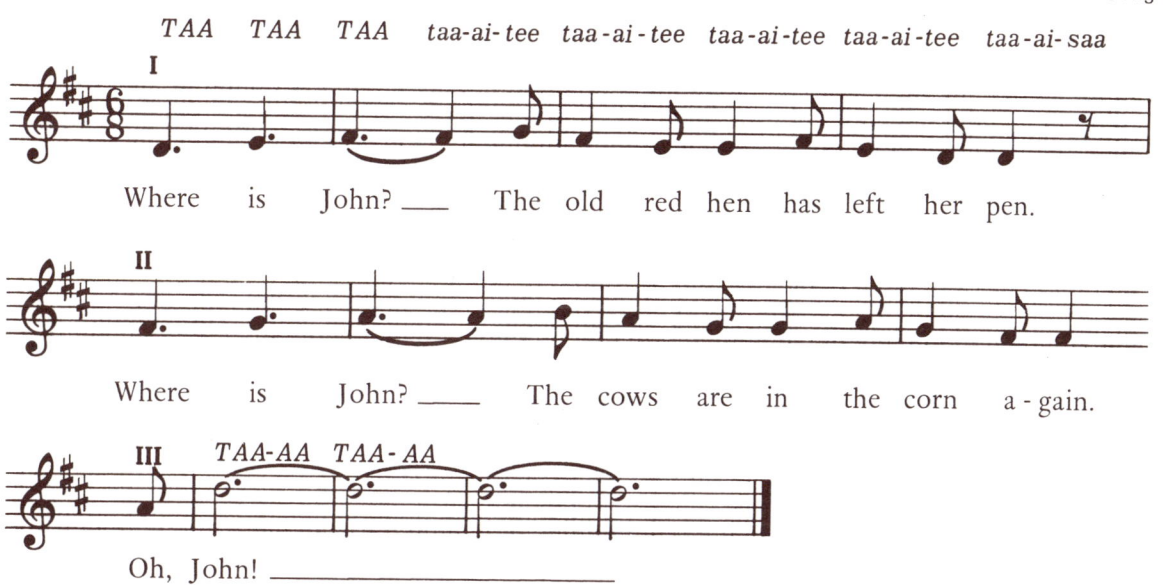

Sing it through to the time names (2 beats to the bar).

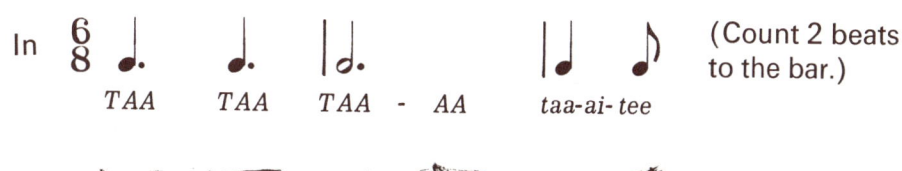

(Count 2 beats to the bar.)

INTERVAL PREPARATION

d' d d' d d'   l   d r d r m d

The Old Woman and the Pedlar

Old English Folk Song

There was an old wo-man as I've heard tell,

Fah - lah did-dle did-dle dee She went to mar-ket her

eggs for to sell Fah - lah did-dle did-dle dee

She went to mar - ket all on a mar-ket day

Fah - lah did-dle did-dle dee But she fell a-sleep on the

king's high - way Fah - lah did-dle did-dle dee.

2. There came along a pedlar, his name was Stout,
    Fah-lah-diddle-diddle-dee
  He cut her petticoats all 'round about, etc.
  He cut her petticoats up to her knees, etc.
  Which made the old woman shiver and sneeze, etc.

3. When this little woman did first awake, etc.
  She began to shiver and she began to shake, etc.
  She began to wonder and she began to cry, etc.
  Deary, deary me, this cannot be I, etc.

4. But if it be I, as I hope it be, etc.
  I've a little dog at home and he'll know me, etc.
  If it be I, he'll wag his tail, etc.
  And if it be not, he will bark and wail, etc.

5. Home went the old woman all in the dark, etc.
  Up got the little dog and he began to bark, etc.
  He began to bark, and she began to cry, etc.
  Oh deary, deary me, this cannot be I, etc.

Dramatize the story with appropriate actions.

Conduct four beats to the bar.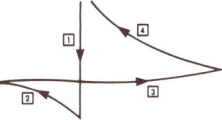

The Bell Doth Toll

English Round

The bell doth toll, its ech-oes roll, I know the sound full well;
I love its ring-ing, For it calls to sing-ing, With its
bim, bim, bim, bom, bell, Bim, bom, bim, bom, bell.

INTERVAL PREPARATION

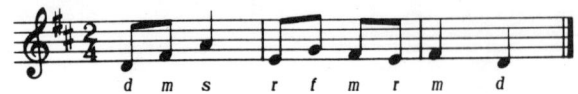

d m s r f m r m d

We Are Musicians

Brightly

German Folk Song

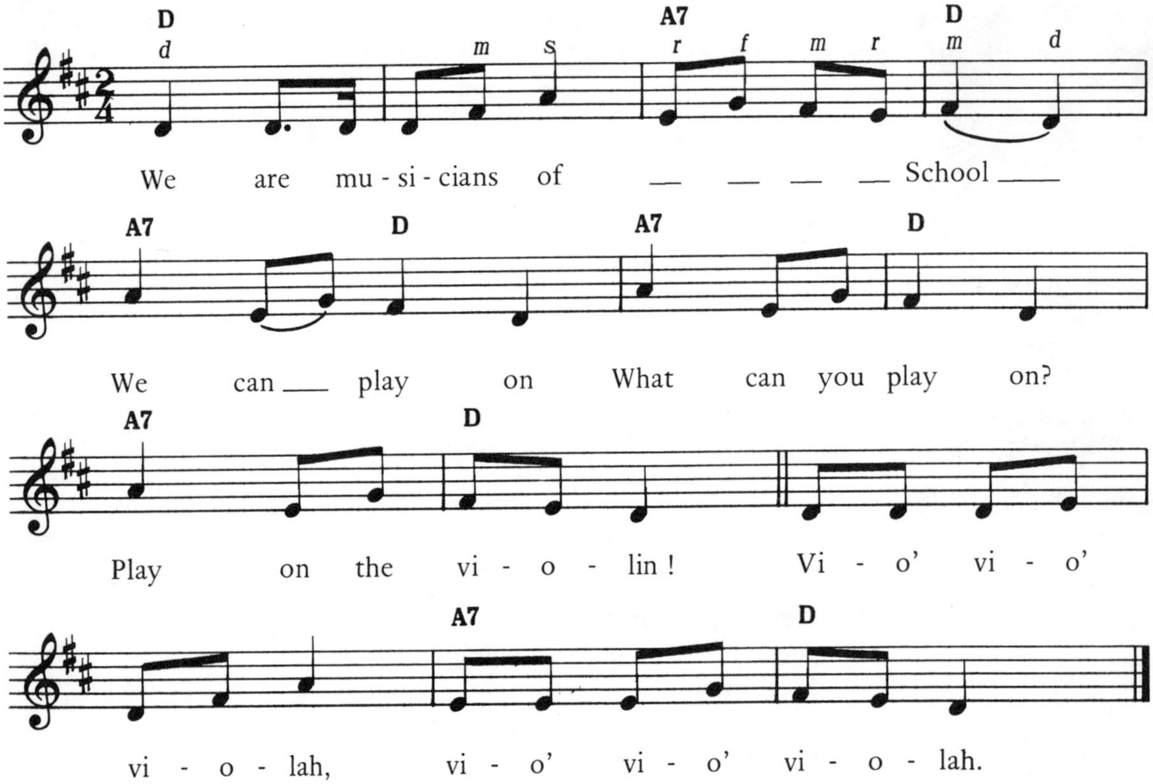

D
d
m s
A7
r f m r
D
m d
We are mu - si - cians of — — — — School —
A7 D A7 D
We can — play on What can you play on?
A7 D
Play on the vi - o - lin! Vi - o' vi - o'
A7 D
vi - o - lah, vi - o' vi - o' vi - o - lah.

2. Bass viol: Zumba zumba zumba zah
3. Piano: Piano piano piano lah
4. Recorder: Tootle tootle tootle tah
5. Autoharp: Strumba strumba strumba zah
6. Tambourine: Tambour-tambour-tamb
7. Bells: Ding dong, ding dong, ding dong bells
8. Telephone: Hello hello hello lah
9. Radio: Super super super suds

ABOUT THE SONG

This is a *cumulative* song. This means that at the end of the second verse, after singing the sounds of the bass viol, you repeat the sounds of the violin; in the third verse, after singing the sounds of the piano, you repeat the sounds of both the bass viol and the violin; and so on until the last verse, in which you sing the sounds of all the instruments. This is an old German folk song, with the words translated into English. It can be made expecially *your* song by simply filling in the name of your school in the first line. If you wish, fill in the name of your class instead (for example, "Grade Four Class", or "Mr. Edward's Class"). Make up actions to suit each instrument.

Sing it to the time names.

Compose additional verses.

Hallow-e'en

Words and Music by
Cyril Mossop

1. I like to dress up on Hallow-e'en,
And wear a funny costume yellow and green,
I like to knock on ev-'ry-one's door,
And call "trick or treat" for candies more!

2. I like to carry a lantern bright,
And *scare* other people with my pumpkin light,
When I get home and open my bag,
To count all the treats down in my sack.

3. Witch-es on broom-sticks they scare me through!
I would-n't want to meet them or taste their brew!
I'm quite con-tent in my cos-tume bright
To knock on man-y doors on Hall-ow-e'en night.

Why does the music sound more "spooky" at the beginning of the third verse?

INTERVAL PREPARATION

m d s   f r l   t l s f m r d

Brother, Come and Dance

Gretel (or all the girls) — "Hansel and Gretel", Humperdinck

Broth-er, come and dance with me, Both my hands I give to thee;

f r l   t l s   f

Right foot first, left foot then, Round a-bout and back a-gain.

Hansel (or all the boys)

m t,

I would dance, but don't know how, When to step and when to bow;

m fe* s r   s l t   d' fe s

Show me what I ought to do And then I'll come and dance with you.

Let your feet go tap, tap, tap, Let your hands go clap, clap, clap;
Let your head go nick, nick, nick, Let your fin-gers click, click, click;

Right foot first, left foot then, Round a-bout and back a-gain.
Right foot first, left foot then, Round a-bout and back a-gain.

* Notice that the tonic sol-fa symbol for B natural is *fe*.

Follow the directions in the words. You will enjoy dancing to this song.
Listen to "Hansel and Gretel", Humperdinck. (Victor Listening Album Four.)

MAJOR SCALES

1. Sing d r m f s l t d'
2. Play this scale of eight tones (an octave) on the bells or piano, beginning on middle C (the home note, sometimes called the tonic note).
3. On the musical staff, C scale will look like this.

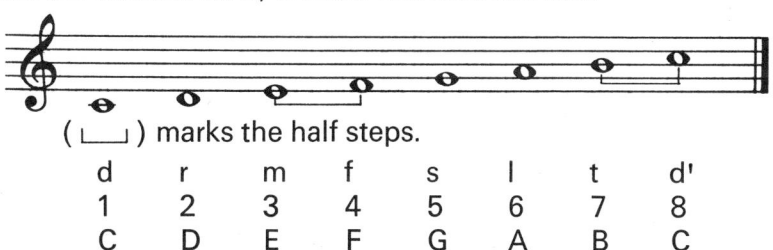

(⌐⌐) marks the half steps.

Now add other kinds of notations and sing them.

d	r	m	f	s	l	t	d'
1	2	3	4	5	6	7	8
C	D	E	F	G	A	B	C

"Some Folks Do" (page 22) uses the notes from the F scale. Doh, or the home tone, is F. There is one flat in the key of F.
On the staff, F scale looks like this. Play it on the piano or bells.

Discover the half steps.

d	r	m	f	s	l	t	d'
1	2	3	4	5	6	7	8
F	G	A	B♭	C	D	E	F

"Fire's Burning" (page 10) uses the notes of the G scale. There is 1 sharp in the G scale. Doh, or the home tone, is G.

Discover the half steps.

d	r	m	f	s	l	t	d'
1	2	3	4	5	6	7	8
G	A	B	C	D	E	F#	G

"The Old Woman and the Pedlar" (page 24), "We Are Musicians" (page 26), and "The Deaf Woman's Courtship" (page 6) use the notes from the scale of D. Doh (the home tone) is D. There are 2 sharps in the key of D.

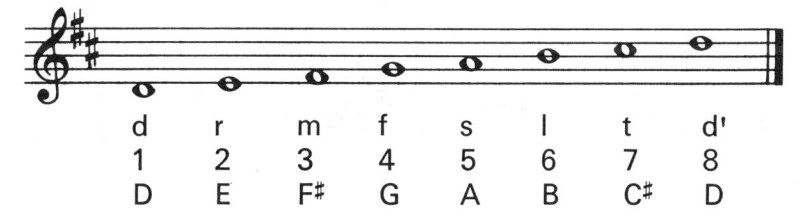

Find the half steps.

d	r	m	f	s	l	t	d'
1	2	3	4	5	6	7	8
D	E	F#	G	A	B	C#	D

MELODY

When you examine familiar melodies on the printed page, you will observe that the melodic line moves up or down by step, skip, or scale. Melodies also make use of repeated notes.

Example 1. Melody built on a scale (step pattern)

(a) from "Brother Come and Dance", page 30.

d' t l s f m r d
8 7 6 5 4 3 2 1

(b) from "Joy to the World"

(c)

from "Rigoletto", by Verdi

Example 2. Melody built on a chord (observe the skips)

from "Simmons", page 4.

Example 3. Melody built on repeated notes

from "My Goose", page 11

Example 4. Melody built on scale, repeated notes, and a skip of an octave

from "For Health and Strength", page 11

By ear and by eye you have recognized that certain phrases in the melody are repeated exactly, while some are repeated note for note but at a higher or lower pitch level. Repetition and sequence are used by most composers to develop variety and interest.

THINGS TO DO Find songs where the melody (1) moves (a) up or (b) down.
(2) uses repeated notes.
(3) is built on a chord.
(4) uses a part of a scale.
(5) uses several of the above characteristics.

Find examples of (a) repeated phrases (b) phrases in sequence

There's a Hole in My Bucket

Lively   Traditional

BOYS: There's a hole in my buck-et, dear Li-za, dear Li-za,

There's a hole in my buck-et, dear Li-za, a hole.

2. Girls: Then mend it, dear Georgie, dear Georgie, etc. . . . mend it.

3. Boys: With what shall I mend it, dear Liza, etc. . . . with what?

4. Girls: With a straw, dear Georgie, dear Georgie, etc. . . . a straw.

5. Boys: If the straw be too long, dear Liza, etc. . . . too long?

6. Girls: Then cut it, dear Georgie, dear Georgie, etc. . . . cut it.

Have fun playing on bells or piano or singing either or both of these chants.

(a)   (b)

ABOUT THE MUSIC

This song uses only five different notes. It is a *pentatonic* tune and can be played entirely on the black keys of the piano or the five black chromatic bars of the bells.

When a song in $\frac{3}{4}$ metre is sung quickly, you *feel* one beat in each bar. Conduct the down beat.
The pattern resembles a half-circle.

THE PENTATONIC SCALE

Most of the songs you will sing are built on a scale of 8 notes.

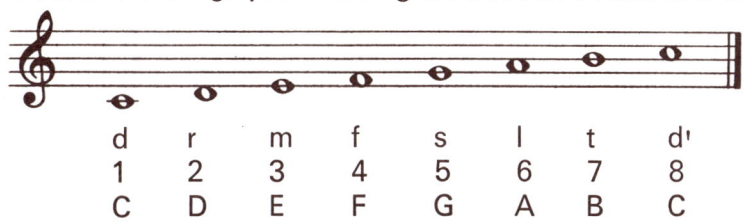

d	r	m	f	s	l	t	d'
1	2	3	4	5	6	7	8
C	D	E	F	G	A	B	C

The pentatonic scale uses only 5 notes. It omits fah and te (4 and 7).

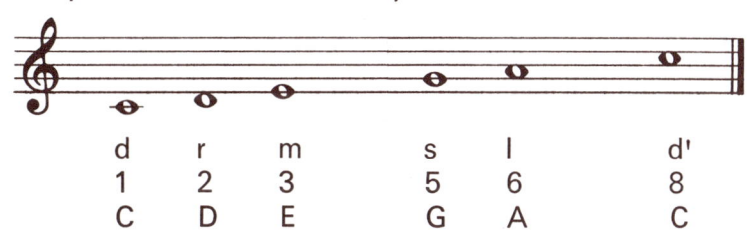

d	r	m	s	l	d'
1	2	3	5	6	8
C	D	E	G	A	C

Many Chinese and Japanese songs, as well as Scottish and American folk songs and spirituals, are pentatonic melodies.

Get to know the *pentatonic sound*. Play the 5-note scale starting on C, D, F♯ (or any other note) on the piano or bells. Half the class sing l d r m s l l s m r d l while the other half listen. Reverse the rôle of listener and singer.

Here is a four-bar pentatonic melody which seems to ask a question. Compose a four-bar melody which will answer the question.

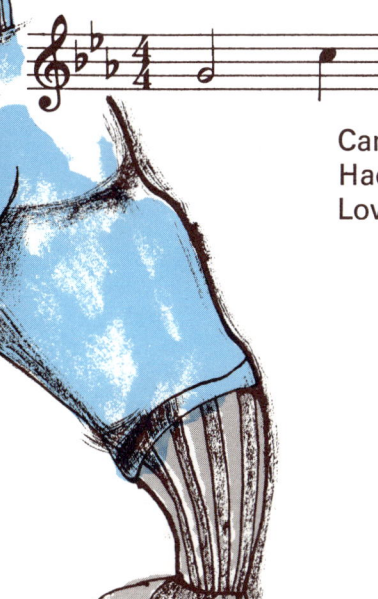

Can you sing these well-known pentatonic songs: "Old MacDonald Had a Farm"; "Li'l Liza Jane"; "Camptown Races"; "Swing Low, Sweet Chariot"?

INTERVAL PREPARATION

d s l s m d m r d l d

Old Texas

Echo Song

Oklahoma Cowboy Song

1. I'm goin' to leave _____ old Tex-as now,
   I'm goin' to leave _____ old Tex-as now,
   They've got no use _____ for the long-horn cow.
   They've got no use _____ for the long-horn cow.

2. They've plowed and fenced my cattle range,
   And the people there are all so strange.

3. I'll take my horse, I'll take my rope,
   And hit the trail upon a lope.

4. Say adios to the Alamo
   And turn my head toward Mexico.

The teacher may sing the first phrase with the class echoing the melody, or the class may be divided into two groups. Group 1 starts and group 2 is the "echo" group. Listen as you sing this pentatonic tune. Be sure to hold notes to full value.

Using the 5th and 6th of the scale we can improvise two simple chants.

clip   clop   clip   clop

Leav-ing   old   Tex - as   Leav - ing   old   Tex - as

Use these chants as a two- or four-bar introduction and coda. (Coconut shells, paper cups, clapping (with a hollow sound) portray the sound of a horse's hooves).

MORE ABOUT SOUND

How many kinds of sound can you get using a piece of paper, a ruler, and an elastic band?

A Little Night Music

Mozart

Wolfgang Mozart (pronounced Mohtzart) was one of the greatest composers of all time. * He lived in Austria nearly two hundred years ago.
One of his best-known pieces he called simply "A Little Night Music" (in German, "Eine Kleine Nachtmusik"). You will find the main tune easy to remember because it starts with doh and continues with soh-doh repeated twice, followed by the I-chord (doh-me-soh). Listen to the first few bars of the record, then sing the tune, using the tonic sol-fa syllables. Mozart wrote his music for string instruments. Listen to the whole first movement (the *allegro* section) to become familiar to the sound of music "for strings".
See if you can hear the main tune that you just sang played again near the end of the piece in exactly the same way as at the beginning.

THE VIOLIN

The violin is the instrument that is used most in the orchestra. It can play about as low as you can sing, but it can also play much higher than your voice.
It has 4 strings that are 5 notes apart: G (the lowest), D, A, and E (the highest). It is usually played with a bow, but sometimes the player plucks the strings with his finger. When he plucks the strings, he is playing *pizzicato*.

* For a detailed story about Mozart and his music, see *Music for Young Listeners* (*The Green Book*), pp. 19–32 Toronto: W. J. Gage, Ltd.

In this quartet, violins combine with a violoncello ('cello for short). At right is a bass viol, the largest of this family of stringed instruments.

THINGS TO DO Bring a violin to look at in class. If any class member is taking lessons on the violin, he might play a short piece. Invite a student from another class if necessary. Listen to a violin record from the following list:

> "Romance", from *A Little Night Music*, by Mozart, in *Adventures in Music*, Grade 5, Vol. 1, R.C.A. Victor.
>
> "Waltz", by Tchaikovsky, in *Adventures in Music*, Grade 5, Vol. 1, R.C.A. Victor.
>
> Violin record in *Meet the Instruments*, Bowmar Records. "Hoe-Down", by Copland, *Bowmar Orchestral Library*, No. 55.
>
> Pantomime from "The Ballet Music to Les Petits Riens", Mozart.

INTERVAL PREPARATION

d' s   m d s   m s   m s f   r f f r d

Amsterdam

Music by Mozart
Words by Anne Ross

In march time

Am - ster - dam is the town that we live in,

Am - ster - dam is the town we be - lieve in.

Sing a song of our ci - ty in Hol - land,

As we march to the sound of the drums;

Sing a song of our ci - ty in Hol - land,

"Am - ster - dam, Am - ster - dam" sing the drums.

40

ABOUT THE MUSIC
This piece is from a comic opera by Mozart called "The Marriage of Figaro". It is sung by Figaro, a barber, to a boy who is joining the army.
It should therefore be sung with vigour, like a march.
It has been given new words to help you remember the sound of ♪♫♩
(Just think of the word "Amsterdam").
How many times does Mozart use the pattern ♪♫♩ in this song?

THINGS TO DO
Sing the song to the time names and clap the ♪♫♩ each time it appears. Be sure to make the middle note (called a sixteenth note) very short!
Sing the song again, changing the rhythm pattern ♪♫♩ to ♫♩ throughout the whole piece. Clap this pattern too, keeping the *two eighths* notes of equal value.
Why do you think that Mozart chose the pattern ♪♫♩ for this song instead of ♫♩?
Now try tapping the dotted eighth and sixteenth notes (♪♫♩) with your left hand while you tap a steady marching beat (equal quarter notes) with your right hand.
Use a drum to this rhythmic pattern:

MUSIC FOR LISTENING
Other Mozart songs that you can sing and play are:
"Alleluia", which appears in Book 6 of this Music Series.
"Minuet", from "The Marriage of Figaro", in *Melody, Rhythm and Harmony*, by L. H. Slind (Mills Music Inc.)
"Minuet", from "The Marriage of Figaro", in *Bowmar Orchestral Library*, No. 53.

INTERVAL PREPARATION

s f m d m m r r d   s l t a l s f m d

Old Joe Clarke

Lively
Tennessee Folk Song

Round and round, Old Joe Clarke, Round and round, I say,
Round and round, Old Joe Clarke, I ain't got long to stay. *Fine*

1. Old Joe Clarke he had a house six-teen sto-ries high,
   D.C. al Fine
   Ev-'ry sto-ry in that house was full of chick-en pie.

2. Old Joe Clarke he had a mule,
   Name was Morgan Brown,
   All the teeth in that mule's head
   Were fifteen inches round.
       Chorus . . .

3. Old Joe Clarke he had a cat,
   Couldn't sing or pray,
   Stuck her head in buttermilk
   And washed her sins away.
       Chorus . . .

D.C. (abbreviation of the Italian "da capo") means "from the beginning".

Fine (pronounced "feenay") means "finish", and marks the end of a verse.

THINGS TO DO	Before you sing the song, look for two rhythmic patterns that you learned in the "Amsterdam" song by Mozart.

Clap bars one and two.

Clap the rhythm of the whole song as you say the words in time.

Now, sing the song after sounding the keynote and the I-chord. |
| **ABOUT THE MUSIC** | There are many versions of this old mountain song which reflects the quaint humour of the times.
Note that in line 3, another flat (♭) is added to the music. Extra sharps and flats that are not in the key signature but appear in the middle of a song are called *accidentals*. They raise or lower notes only in the bar in which they are written.
Listen to the sound of the accidentals in "Old Joe Clarke", and then try playing the song on bells without the accidentals. Notice how the E♭ accidental gives the piece more colour. |
| **MORE THINGS TO DO** | 1. Make up a "Virginia Reel" type of square dance to go with the music of "Old Joe Clarke".
2. Make up additional verses to the song. |
| **MUSIC FOR LISTENING** | "Desert Water Hole", by Grofé, in *Adventures in Music*, Grade 4, Vol. 1. |

INTERVAL PREPARATION

d d m r d t l s r r d e r m r d

Who Did Swallow Jonah?

Dialogue Song

Spiritual (arr. Earle Terry)

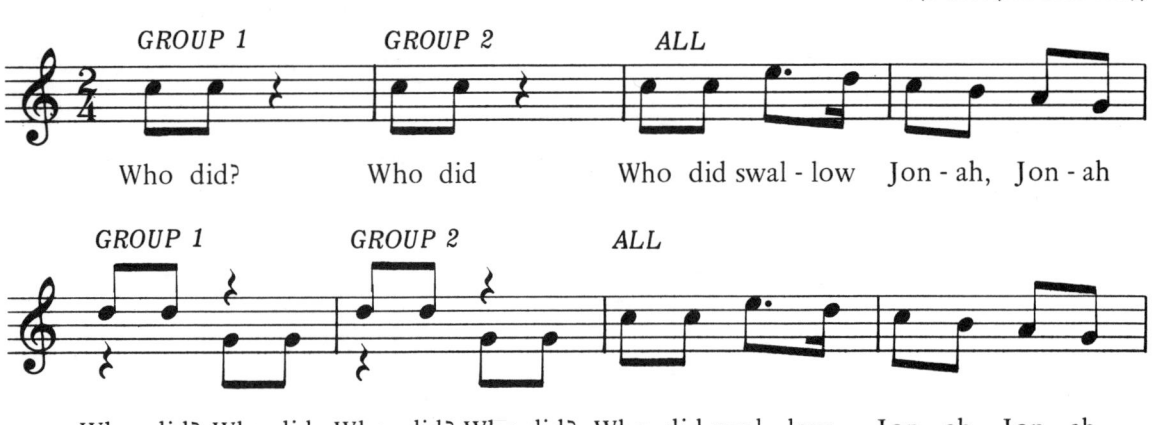

GROUP 1: Who did?
GROUP 2: Who did
ALL: Who did swal-low Jon-ah, Jon-ah

GROUP 1: Who did? Who did
GROUP 2: Who did? Who did?
ALL: Who did swal-low Jon-ah, Jon-ah

GROUP 1: Who did? Who did?
GROUP 2: Who did? Who did?
ALL: Who did? swal-low Jon-ah Jon-ah

Who did swal-low Jon - ah U ——————— P!

2. Whale did, whale did. Whale did swallow Jonah, Jonah.
   Whale did swallow Jonah up!

3. Daniel, Daniel, Dan-iel in the li-on, li-on,
   Daniel in the lion's den.

4. Gabriel, Gabriel, Gabriel blow your trump, trump, trump, trump,
   Gabriel blow your trumpet loud.

44

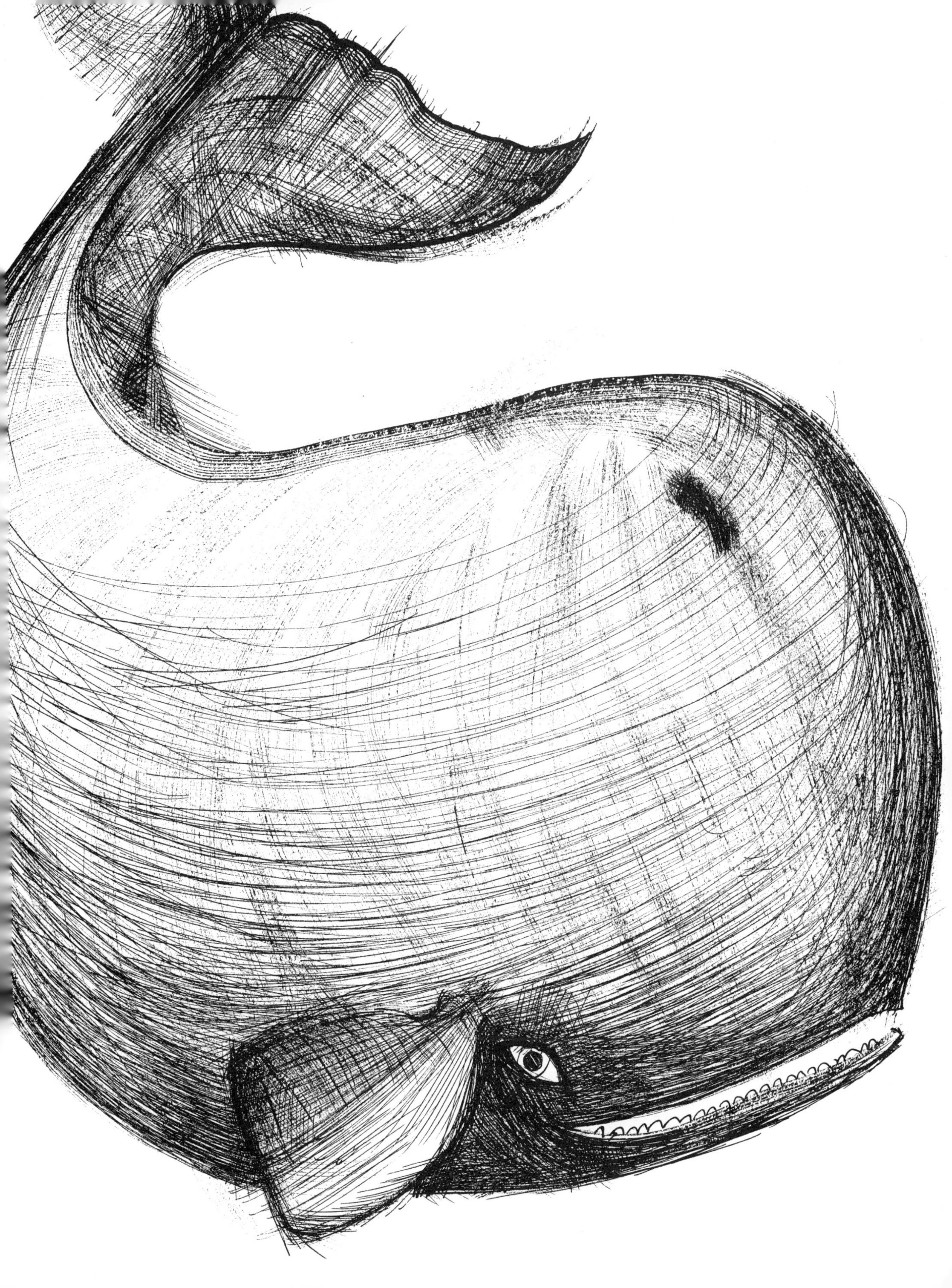

INTERVAL PREPARATION

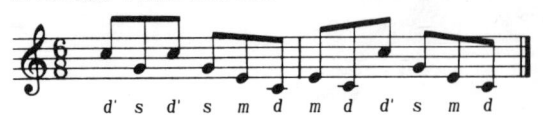

d' s d' s m d m d d' s m d

Oliver Cromwell

Old English Folk Song

Oli-ver Crom-well lay bur-ied and dead,
Hee - haw, bur-ied and dead.
There grew an old cher-ry tree o-ver his head,
Hee haw o-ver his head. (The)

2. The cherries were ripe—and ready to fall,
   Hee-haw, ready to fall.
   There came an old lady to gather them all,
   Hee-haw, gather them all.

3. Oliver rose—and gave her a drop,
   Hee-haw, gave her a drop,
   Which made the old lady go hippity hop,
   Hee-haw, hippity-hop.

4. The saddle and bridle they lie on the shelf,
   Hee-haw, lie on the shelf.
   If you want any more you can sing it yourself,
   Hee-haw, sing it yourself!

ABOUT THE SONG

This is an old English song about Oliver Cromwell, the stern man who ruled England for a short time in the seventeenth century, after King Charles I was beheaded and there was temporarily no king or queen. There are several versions of this song. This is quite usual in folk music.

ABOUT
THE MUSIC

This is a song that is made up entirely from the I-chord. Sing the song once, using the numbers of the scale (1 1 1 5 5 5 3 3 3 1, etc.) instead of words. Now sing the song to the syllables.
Do you remember a song in this book that could be accompanied by just the I-chord? Sing it!

There is something new about the rhythm of this piece. Note that three eighth notes are grouped together rather than the usual group of two eighth notes.

The $\frac{6}{8}$ at the beginning of the music tells us that there are six counts in a measure and an eighth note gets 1 count.
At a fast tempo you feel and hear the six-note pattern as two groups of three. The strong beat (primary) falls on the first eighth note and the weak beat (secondary) falls on the fourth note, creating two beats to the bar.

RHYTHM OF THE MELODY

RHYTHM OF THE BEAT

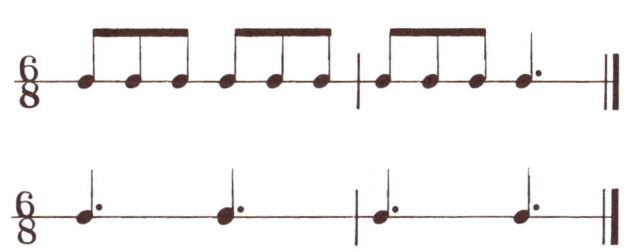

Using different instruments, combine the rhythm of the melody and the rhythm of the beat, while a group of students chant the words. When you sing $\frac{6}{8}$ quickly, conduct as in $\frac{2}{4}$.

THINGS TO DO

Sing the song with a small group taking the solo part and the whole class singing the chorus part.
Dramatize the text.

47

Dashing Away with the Smoothing Iron

English Folk Song

'Twas on a Mon-day morn—-ing when I be-held my dar—-ling,

She look'd so neat and charm—-ing in ev-'ry high de-gree;

She look'd so neat and nim-ble, Oh! A-wash-ing of her lin-en, Oh!

Dash-ing a-way with the smooth-ing iron,

Dash-ing a-way with the smooth-ing iron,

She stole my heart a-way.

Tuesday . . . A-starching
Wednesday . . . A-hanging
Thursday . . . A-ironing
Friday . . . A-folding
Saturday . . . A-airing
Sunday . . . A-wearing

This is a fun song. Act out each verse.
Clap 2 beats to the bar. Conduct

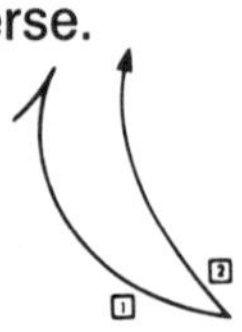

RHYTHM

People speak of "keeping" or "beating" time to music they hear. Musicians speak of the *rhythm of the beat* (or of the pulse).

Clap as you sing this tune. As you feel the rhythm, you will find the beats fall into groups of two.

Clap the *rhythm of the beat* again, accenting the first beat behind each bar line.

RHYTHM OF THE BEAT

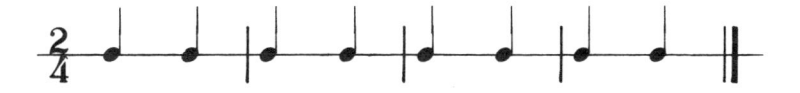

Chanting the words that go with this melody will help you discover the *rhythm of the melody*.

RHYTHM OF THE MELODY

RHYTHM OF THE WORDS: Why should-n't my goose sing as well as your goose.

Now combine the rhythm of the melody with the rhythm of the beat. Later, add a third rhythm of the accompaniment.

RHYTHM OF THE MELODY

RHYTHM OF THE BEAT

RHYTHM OF THE ACCOMPANIMENT

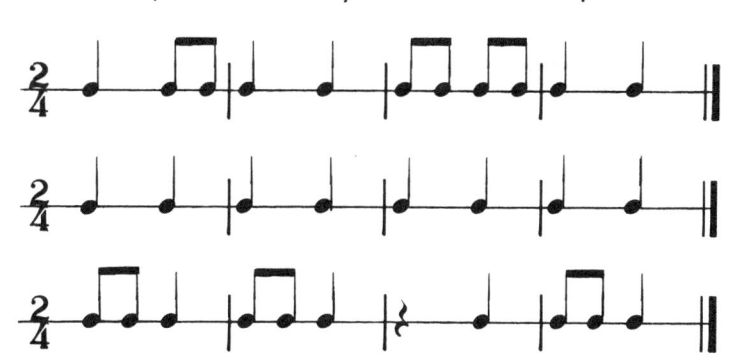

Play the rhythm of the beat on a drum. Choose appropriate instruments for the accompaniment. Sing or play the melody on the piano or bells. Create a new rhythmic accompaniment.

Conduct $\frac{2}{4}$, two beats to the bar.

INTERVAL PREPARATION

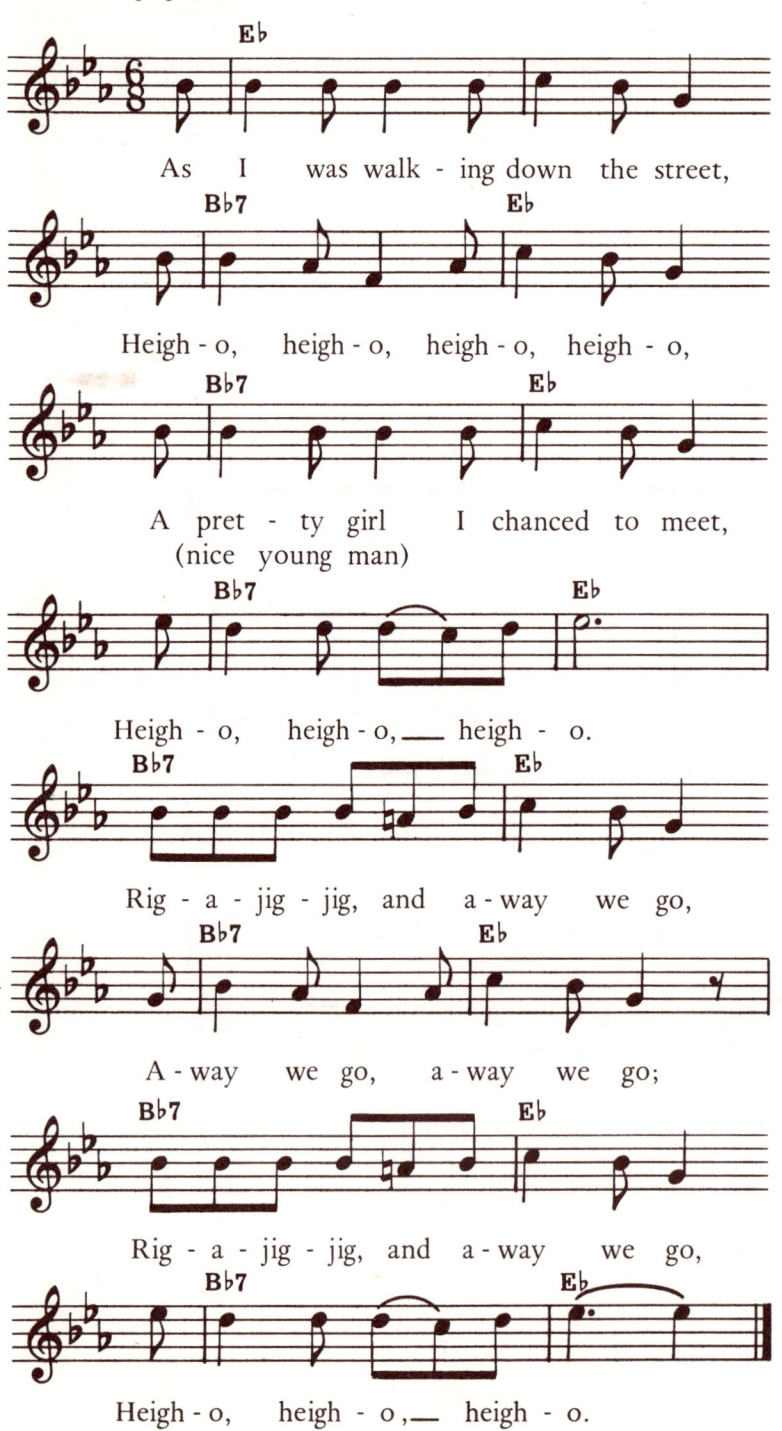

s s l s m s r f l s m s f e s l s m d

Rig-a-Jig-Jig
Singing Game

As I was walk-ing down the street,

Heigh-o, heigh-o, heigh-o, heigh-o,

A pret-ty girl I chanced to meet,
(nice young man)

Heigh-o, heigh-o, heigh-o.

Rig-a-jig-jig, and a-way we go,

A-way we go, a-way we go;

Rig-a-jig-jig, and a-way we go,

Heigh-o, heigh-o, heigh-o.

Conduct 2 beats to the bar:

While group 1 plays the rhythm on a drum, group 2 plays the rhythm below on another instrument:

Suggest other persons one might meet on the street (policeman, postman, etc.)

Create a dance. For example: Form a circle. All sing. One boy goes to the centre. The circle skips about the boy who selects a partner at the words, "a pretty girl". The partners join hands and skip around inside the circle in the opposite direction to which the circle is moving. When the song is repeated the couple separate and the boy chooses a new partner, and the dance continues until all have had an opportunity to skip around inside the circle.

Here is the E flat scale.

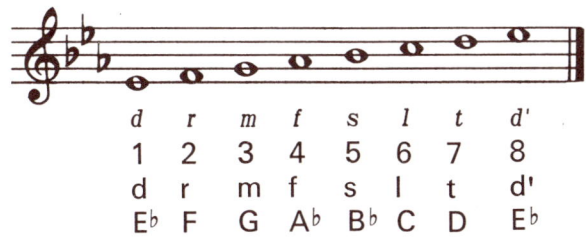

d	r	m	f	s	l	t	d'
1	2	3	4	5	6	7	8
d	r	m	f	s	l	t	d'
E♭	F	G	A♭	B♭	C	D	E♭

INTERVAL PREPARATION

d m m r d r r d s, s f m m d

Ah! Si Mon Moine Voulait Danser

Lively French-Canadian Folk Song

Ah! si mon moi - ne vou - lait dan - ser,
Oh! would you like to_____ dance with me,

Ah! si mon moi - ne vou - lait dan - ser,
Oh! would you like to_____ dance with me,

Un ca - pu - chon je lui don - ner - ais,
A bright new cap I will give you free,

Un ca - pu - chon je lui don - ner - ais.
A bright new cap I will give you free.

Dan - se mon moine dan - se,
Dance now let us dance now,

Tu n'en - tends pas la dan - se;
This is your per - fect chance now;

Tu n'en - tends pas mon mou - lin, lon, la,
Oh! would you like to_____ dance with me,

Tu n'en - tends pas mon mou - lin, lon, la.
A bright new cap I will give you free.

52

Make up more verses of your own, replacing "A bright new cap" with other words such as "A diamond ring" or "A new red dress", etc.

This song is a favorite in Quebec. Try singing the French words.

ABOUT THE MUSIC

The distance between the first two notes is the same as in "Fire's Burning" and "A Little Night Music". Sing the first bar of "Fire's Burning". Now you can sing the first two notes of this new piece! In music, we use the word *interval* to describe the distance between any two notes.

The interval between the first two notes of this song is called an interval of a 4th because the notes are four notes apart, counting the bottom note as the first. Sing d r m f, then sing d f. Play this interval on the bells. Can you recall a popular Christmas carol that starts d f?

Which phrases are alike? What is the mood of this song?

Find and clap these rhythmic patterns in the song.

Which instruments are most appropriate for accompaniment?

REVIEW 1

1. In your notebook, write the time names for the notes in (a) and (b) below:

   (a) [musical notation in 2/4]

   (b) [musical notation in 4/4]

2. In your notebook, write the tonic sol-fa symbols for the notes in (a) and (b) below.

   (a) [musical notation in 4/4, two flats]

   (b) [musical notation in 2/4]

3. These rhythmic patterns come from songs you have learned. Can you name the songs? (Tap or clap the rhythm first.)

   Example:

   [rhythmic notation in 2/4]

   Answer — "Brother, Come and Dance".

   Try these:

   (a) [rhythmic notation in 4/4]

   (b) [rhythmic notation in 2/4]

   (c) [rhythmic notation in 6/8]

Bonavist' Harbour

Brightly
Newfoundland

Lots of fish in Bon-a-vist' Har-bour,

Lots of fish-er-men there.

Swing your part-ner, Jim-my Joe Ja-cobs,

I'll be home in the spring of the year.

CHORUS

Catch hold this one, Swing a-round that one,

Catch hold this one, Did-dle dum dee,

Catch hold this one, Swing a-round that one,

Swing a-round this one, Catch hold that one,

Tra la la la la la la.

Christmas in Many Lands

Children around the world sing special songs at Christmas. These songs, usually about Jesus' birth, are called *carols*. You may want to make up a story to connect the songs on the following pages for a Christmas party or program.

Beside Thy Cradle Here I Stand

Johann Sebastian Bach

Be - side Thy cra - dle here I stand, O Thou that ev - er liv - est,

And bring Thee with a will - ing hand The ver - y gifts Thou giv - est.

Ac - cept me; 'tis my mind and heart, My soul, my strength, my ev - 'ry part,

That Thou from me re - quir - est.

The melody is from "Christmas Oratorio" composed by Bach in 1734.

Deck the Halls

Gaily   Wales

Deck the halls with boughs of hol-ly,
Fa la la la la, la la la la;
'Tis the sea-son to be jol-ly,
Fa la la la la, la la la la;
Don we now our gay ap-par-el,
Fa la la, la la la, la la la;
Troll the an-cient yule-tide car-ol,
Fa la la la la, la la la la.

2. See the blazing yule before us, Fa la la la la, la la la la;
   Strike the harp and join the chorus, Fa la la la la, la la la la;
   Follow me in merry measure, Fa la la la la la, la la la;
   Heedless of the wind and weather, Fa la la la la, la la la la.

Dance Carol

Sweden

Introduction:

La la la la, la la la la, la la la la,

Melody:

La la la la. Christ-mas is here, Christ-mas is here,

Now the hol-ly leaf is green-o! East-er would come when

Christ-mas is done if Lent did-n't fall be-tween-o!

La la la la la la la!

You will recognize the dotted rhythm ♪♪♪ in this piece. Remember the rhythm of the word "Amsterdam"?

Dance Carol is in the key of A major. There are 3 sharps in this key.

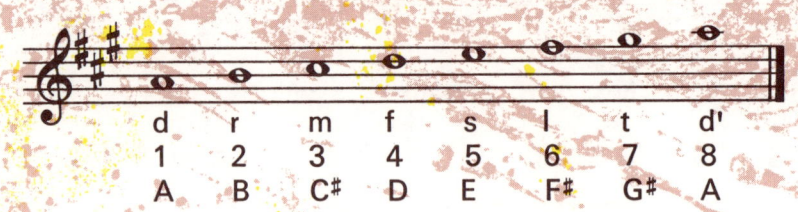

d	r	m	f	s	l	t	d'
1	2	3	4	5	6	7	8
A	B	C#	D	E	F#	G#	A

MUSIC FOR LISTENING

"Shepherd's Dance" from "Amahl and the Night Visitors", by Menotti; *Adventures in Music*, Grade 4, Vol. 2.

Fum Fum Fum

Spanish Dance Carol from Catalonia

Christ - mas day is here once more, sing Fum Fum Fum! ——
Christ - mas day is here once more, sing Fum Fum Fum! Je - sus
Christ was born this day, let us be gay, let us be
gay, Born of Mar - y in a man - ger, bring - ing
joy to friend and stran - ger, Fum Fum Fum!

*Pronounced "Foom Foom Foom", rhyming with "loom".

Add classroom instruments to the words "Fum Fum Fum" each time they appear. What instruments do you think would be most suitable for this song? Note the effect of the change to ¾ time in the last line.

What is the mood of this carol?
Fum Fum Fum is in the key of A minor.

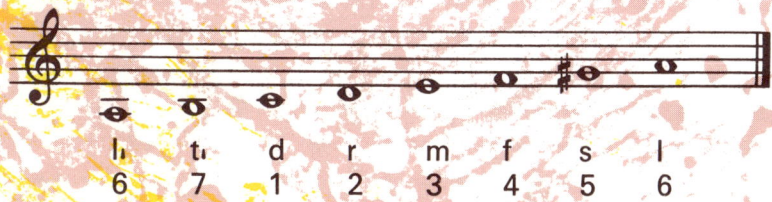

l₁	t₁	d	r	m	f	s	l
6	7	1	2	3	4	5	6

Echo Carol

Germany

1. While by my sheep I watched at night,
2. There shall be born, so he did say

Glad tidings brought an angel bright.
In Bethlehem a child today.

How great my joy, Great my joy,

Joy! Joy! Joy! Joy! Joy! Joy!

Praise we the Lord in heav'n on high,

Praise we the Lord in heav'n on high.

Echo parts may be sung by a small group.
Do you remember the meaning of *mf* and *pp*?

Christmas Is Here

Gaily
Bohemia

Come, let us all be mer-ry for
Ding   Dong

Christ-mas is here! Come, let us all be
Sing the bells! Ding

mer-ry for Christ-mas is here!
Dong   Ring the bells!

Let bells be ring-ing, chil-dren sing-ing; Let bells be ring-ing,
Ding   Dong   Ding

chil-dren sing-ing, Christ-mas is here!
Dong   Ring the bells!

Patapan

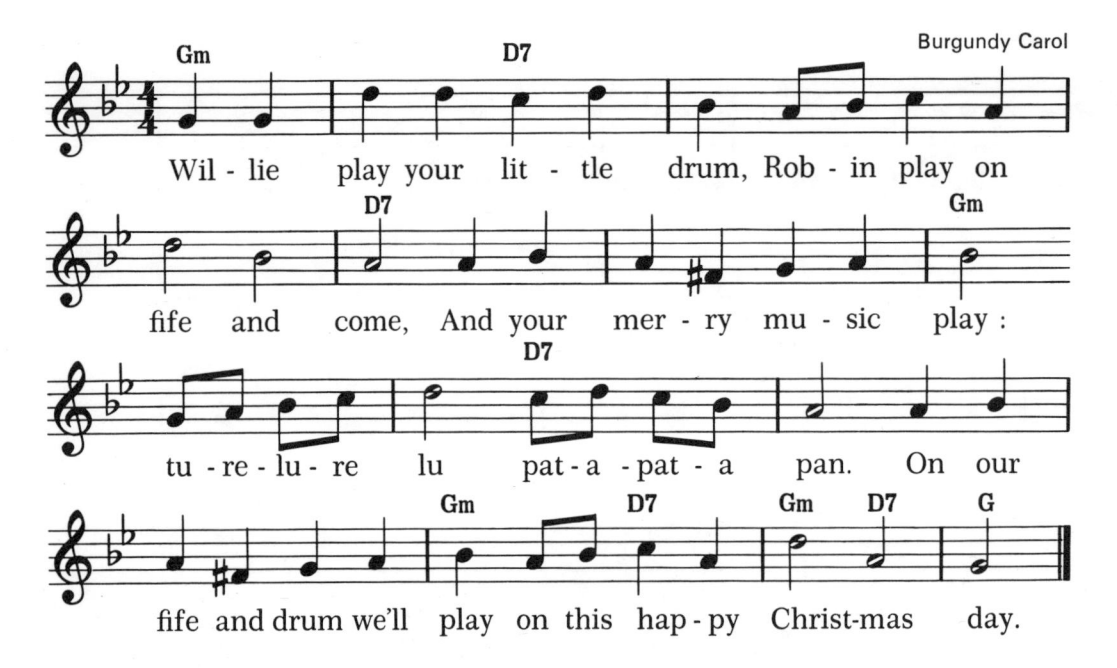

Burgundy Carol

Willie play your little drum, Robin play on fife and come, And your merry music play: tu-re-lu-re lu pat-a-pat-a pan. On our fife and drum we'll play on this happy Christmas day.

Discover the mood of this carol.
Discover the scale pattern and play it on bells.
A drum accompaniment to the rhythm of the word "Pat-a-pan" adds interest.

"Patapan" is in the scale of G minor.

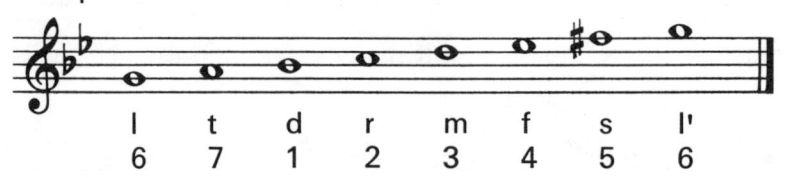

l	t	d	r	m	f	s	l'
6	7	1	2	3	4	5	6

Play and sing this scale.

My Candles

Slowly

Song from Israel

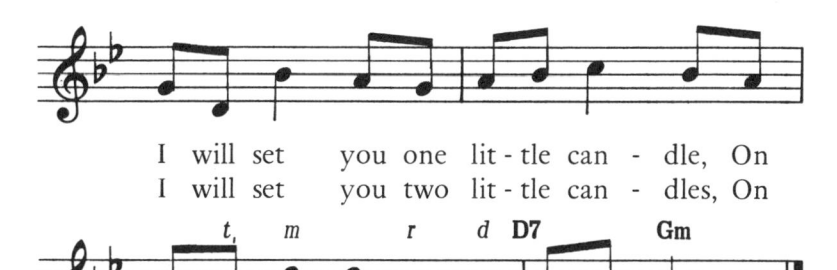

1. In the win-dow where you can send your glow from my Me-no-rah on new-ly fal-len snow, I will set you one lit-tle can-dle, On this the first*__ night of Ha-nuk-kah.
2. In the win-dow where you can send your glow from my Me-no-rah on new-ly fal-len snow, I will set you two lit-tle can-dles, On this the sec-ond night of Ha-nuk-kah.

Hanukkah is the Jewish Festival of Lights, which occurs at the same time as the Christian celebration of Christmas. This Jewish tradition dates back to 165 B.C. During Hanukkah a candle is lighted on the Menorah or candelabra each evening. The ceremony is only complete when eight candles are burning.

On each of the nights of Hanukkah, sing the correct number of candles.

INTERVAL PREPARATION

d r r,t, r t, l,s, r r s,s, d m r d

Michael Finnigin

Traditional

There was a chap called Mi-chael Fin-ni-gin,
He grew whis-kers on his chin-i-gin.
The wind came up and blew them in-i-gin,
Poor old Mi-chael Fin-ni-gin! Be-gin-i-gin: There

Last time
Fin-ni-gin!

The sign :|| in music tells us to "begin-i-gin" or in other words repeat back to the sign ||:
The sign > means accent these notes!

Sing the song to the tonic sol-fa.

Play on piano or bells, or sing this one-note descant *.

Mi-chael Fin-ni-gin Mi-chael Fin-ni-gin Mi-chael Fin-ni-gin

* A "descant" is a tune added above the main melody, usually sung or played by a small group.

As you sing one verse the teacher will write a musical sign on the board telling you how to sing the next verse. She will use some of these signs, which are the abbreviations of the Italian words shown beside them.

    f (*forte*) — loud
mf (*mezzo-forte*) — not quite as loud as "f"
ff (*fortissimo*) — very loud
    p (*piano*) — soft
mp (*mezzo-piano*) — not as soft as "p"
pp (*pianissimo*) — very soft

Follow the signs!
What is the first interval in the piece?
What is the pattern of the three bracketed notes in the first line?
Can you find the same pattern elsewhere in this song?

THINGS TO DO   Notice the rhythm of the melody and the rhythm of the beat.
Compose some more verses for this song and copy them in your notebook.
Keep a separate page in your notebook to collect musical terms like the ones above. What other terms or symbols have you learned thus far? Add these to your list.

Come Let's Dance

A Round

13th-century France

Come, let's dance and sing a song to-geth-er.
Come, we'll laugh and have a jol-ly time.

INTERVAL PREPARATION

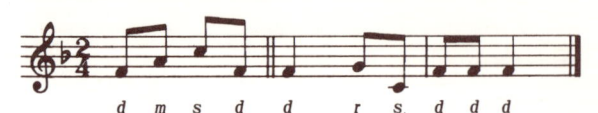

d m s d d r s, d d d

The Greedy Girl

Lively

Slovak Folk Song

Down she sat and loud she cried,
Ay, ay, loud she cried,
"Hung-er I can not a-bide,
Ay, ay, not a-bide."

2. Bread they baked an oven full,
   Ay, ay, oven full;
   Down she sat and ate it all,
   Ay, ay, ate it all.

3. Then two sheep they roasted well,
   Ay, ay, roasted well;
   Down she gulped them hoof and bell,
   Ay, ay, hoof and bell.

4. She could never get her fill,
   Ay, ay, get her fill;
   There she sits, she's eating still,
   Ay, ay, eating still.

ABOUT THE MUSIC

Only two chords are needed to accompany this song. The first chord, the I-chord, was used to accompany "Oliver Cromwell", on page 46. The new chord is called the "five-seven" chord and is written this way: V7-chord.

On the staff, the V7-chord looks like this:

Using the I-chord and the V7-chord, accompany the song on the autoharp. Notation of the rhythm of the first four bars of "The Greedy Girl" looks like this:

In blank notation the rhythm looks like this:

Choose a song and write the rhythm in blank notation.

Here is a musical graph or contour showing the melody of the first two phrases of "The Greedy Girl":

Write the contour of the last two lines.

67

Canoe Song

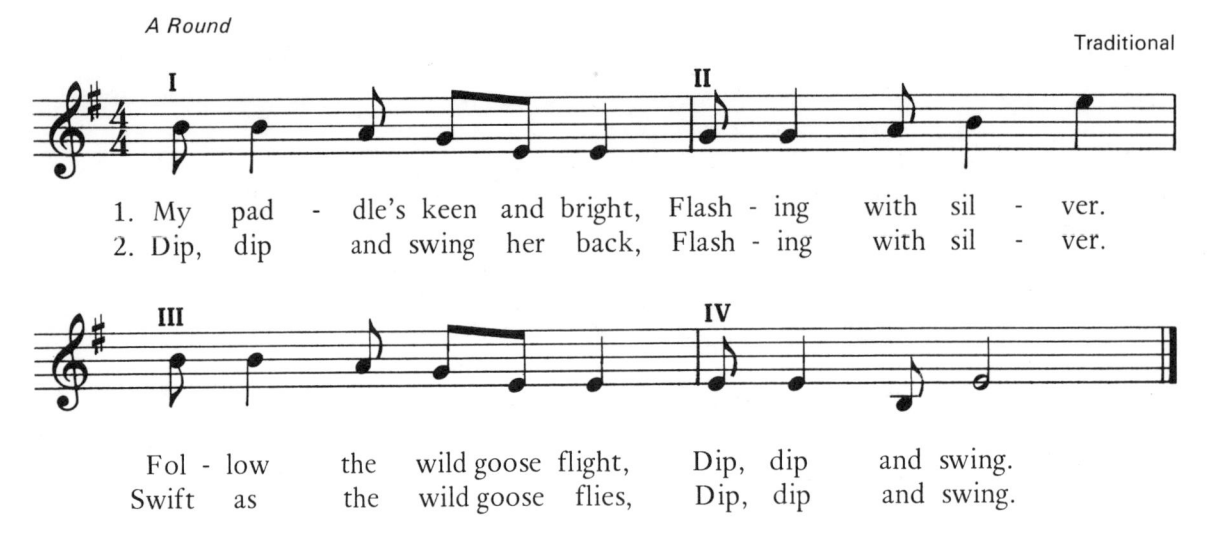

A Round

Traditional

1. My paddle's keen and bright, Flashing with silver.
2. Dip, dip and swing her back, Flashing with silver.

Follow the wild goose flight, Dip, dip and swing.
Swift as the wild goose flies, Dip, dip and swing.

ABOUT THE MUSIC

The pentatonic scale is used in many songs of the North American Indian. Although "My Paddle's Keen and Light" is not originally an Indian song, it has an Indian flavour.

The song beats of this song do not always come at the beginning of the bar where we would expect to find a strong beat. We call this kind of rhythm *syncopation*. Other songs using syncopation are: "Nobody Knows the Trouble I've Seen" and "Jacob's Ladder". Can you sing them?

The scale of E minor looks like this on the staff:

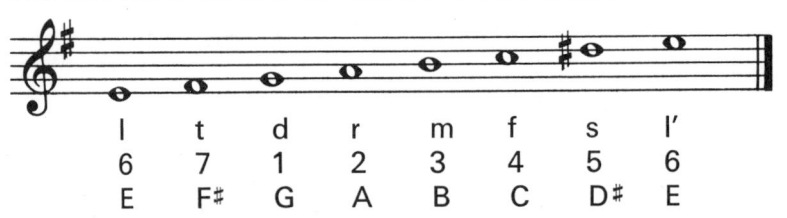

l	t	d	r	m	f	s	l'
6	7	1	2	3	4	5	6
E	F#	G	A	B	C	D#	E

THINGS TO DO

Sing the song using the words.
After the song has been learned, try it as a two-part round.
Use the last bar as a chant.

Dip, dip and swing, dip, dip and swing

68

Use the same chant as a four-bar introduction and coda. Vary the dynamics from *pp* to *f* and vice versa.
The chant can also be played on the piano or bells.
Ask a small group to sing a single-note descant.

Dip,   swing.   Dip,   swing.

This descant can also be effective on bells or piano.
Write the rhythm in blank notation.

SYNCOPATION

Syncopation is a special kind of uneven rhythm in which the accent comes at an unexpected place, bringing a lively excitement to the music.
Discover how it *feels* against the regular rhythm of the beat.
Tap your foot to this rhythm:

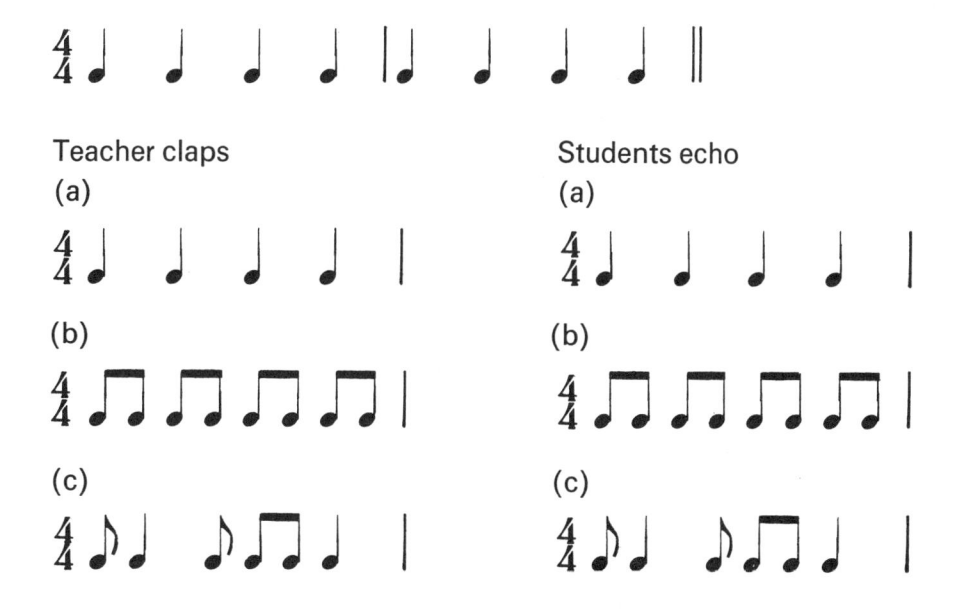

Teacher claps
(a)

Students echo
(a)

(b)

(b)

(c)

(c)

Find the syncopation pattern in "New River Train", page 70.
Notice in "Mañana" (page 71) syncopation is created by the tie which holds the tone across the bar line. We miss the expected accent usually heard on the first beat because of the tie.

INTERVAL PREPARATION

m m s l s m r r m f f e s s s f r d

New River Train

American Folk Song

I'm rid-in' that New Riv-er train, _____ I'm rid-in' that New Riv-er train, _____ The same old train that brought me here, Gon-na car-ry me home a-gain. _____

Using the roots of the chords we create a second part.

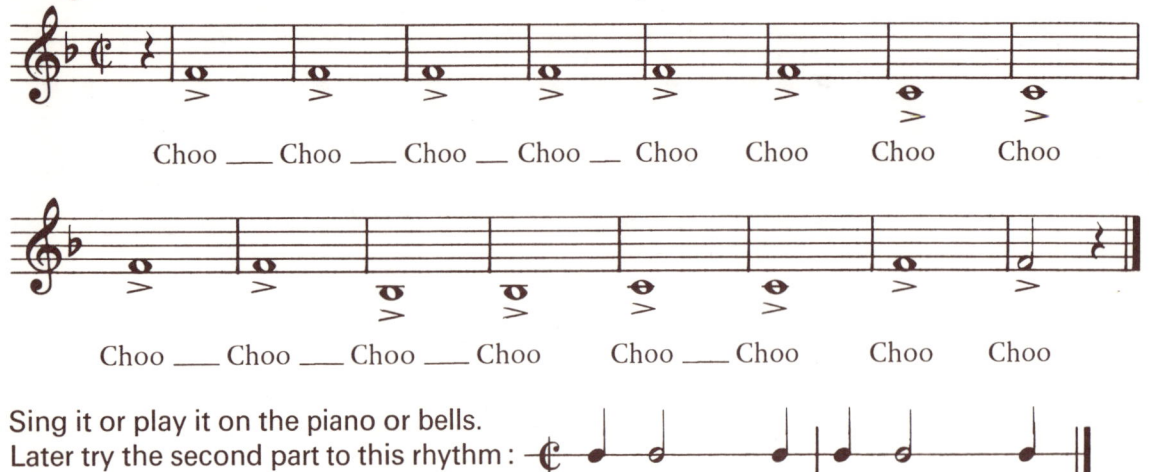

Choo ___ Choo ___ Choo ___ Choo ___ Choo   Choo   Choo   Choo

Choo ___ Choo ___ Choo ___ Choo   Choo ___ Choo   Choo   Choo

Sing it or play it on the piano or bells.
Later try the second part to this rhythm:

Now create your own rhythm for the accompaniment.

INTERVAL PREPARATION

s, d m s d d t, l, s, t, r s,

Mañana

Spanish Folk Song

Ma - ña - na, por la ma - ña - na pa - sas - te,
Jua - na, por mi ta - ller, la ran le. Te
ju - ro que ten - go ga - na de ver - te,
Jua - na, la pun - ta el pie.

Clap the syncopation. Tap your foot to the rhythm of the beat.
When you know the song, learn the descant from the notation.

71

An Eskimo Lullaby

Still now and hear my sing - ing,
Though she as yet knows noth - ing,

Sleep through the night, my Dar - ling. *Fine*
She is so sweet I'm sing - ing.

We have a ti - ny daugh - ter,

Thanks be to God who sent her. *D.C.*

2. Though she as yet knows nothing,
   She is so sweet I'm singing.
   We have a tiny daughter,
   Thanks be to God who sent her.

RHYTHM This is the rhythm of the coffee percolator. Play it on a drum, or tap it with a pen.

Use this rhythm to compose an eight-bar song.
Can you discover and notate another rhythm heard in your classroom?

INTERVAL PREPARATION

s l s m f r s d' s m r d

My Hat It Has Three Corners

German Folk Song

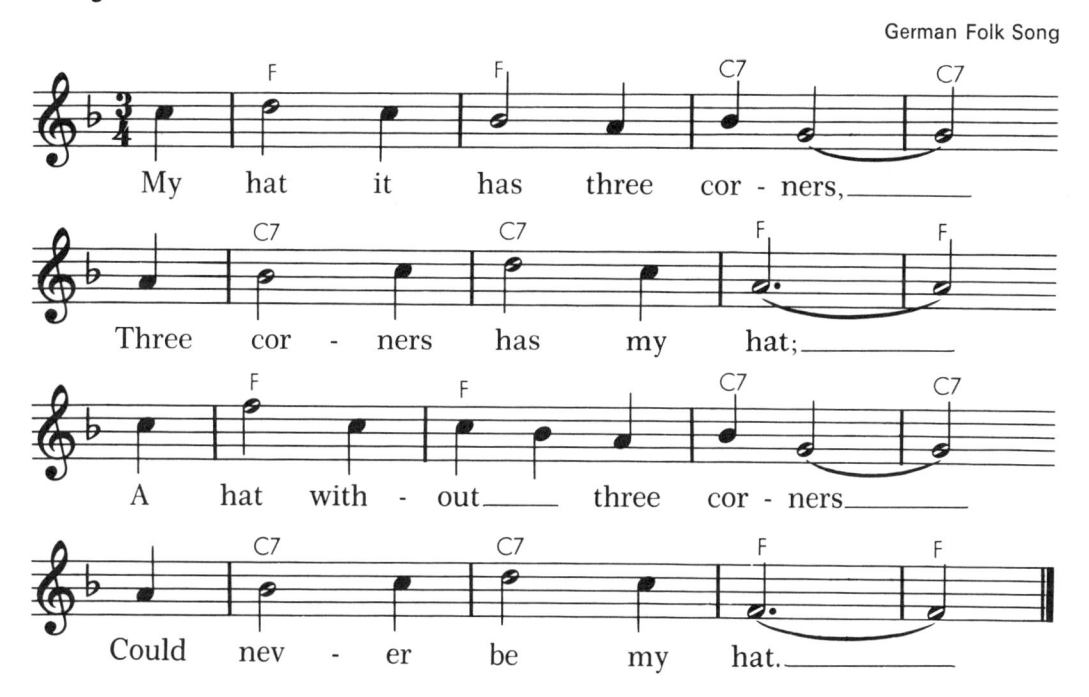

My hat it has three cor - ners,
Three cor - ners has my hat;
A hat with - out three cor - ners
Could nev - er be my hat.

This is another song that you can accompany with the I- and V7-chords. Review the I- and V7-chords as played in "The Greedy Girl", on page 66.

THINGS TO DO Find and play the chords below on the autoharp and bells.

F-chord
I-chord

C7-chord
V7-chord

73

The Cricket Takes a Wife

Vivace
Hungarian Folk Song

1. O the cricket weds to-day, the mosquito's daughter.
Shuffling comes the little louse, best man to the bridegroom;
Hopping comes the nimble flea, for to be the bridesmaid.
Animals both great and small come as guests invited.

Copyright 1956, by Novello & Company Limited

2. Second fiddler is the stork, with the turkey leading;
   Hornets play the double-bass; froggy is the flautist.
   Merrily the monkey jumps, dancing to the polka;
   While that rogue, the old screech-owl, plays upon the bagpipe.

3. And the wolf, the butcher-man, felled six big fat oxen;
   And not satisfied with that, smothered fifty piglets.
   Then the goat she capered in, cooked a tasty goulash.
   But before the meal was served, lo! the cricket vanished.

M.K.

What is the key of this song?
Discover phrases which are alike.
Vivace means lively, spirited.

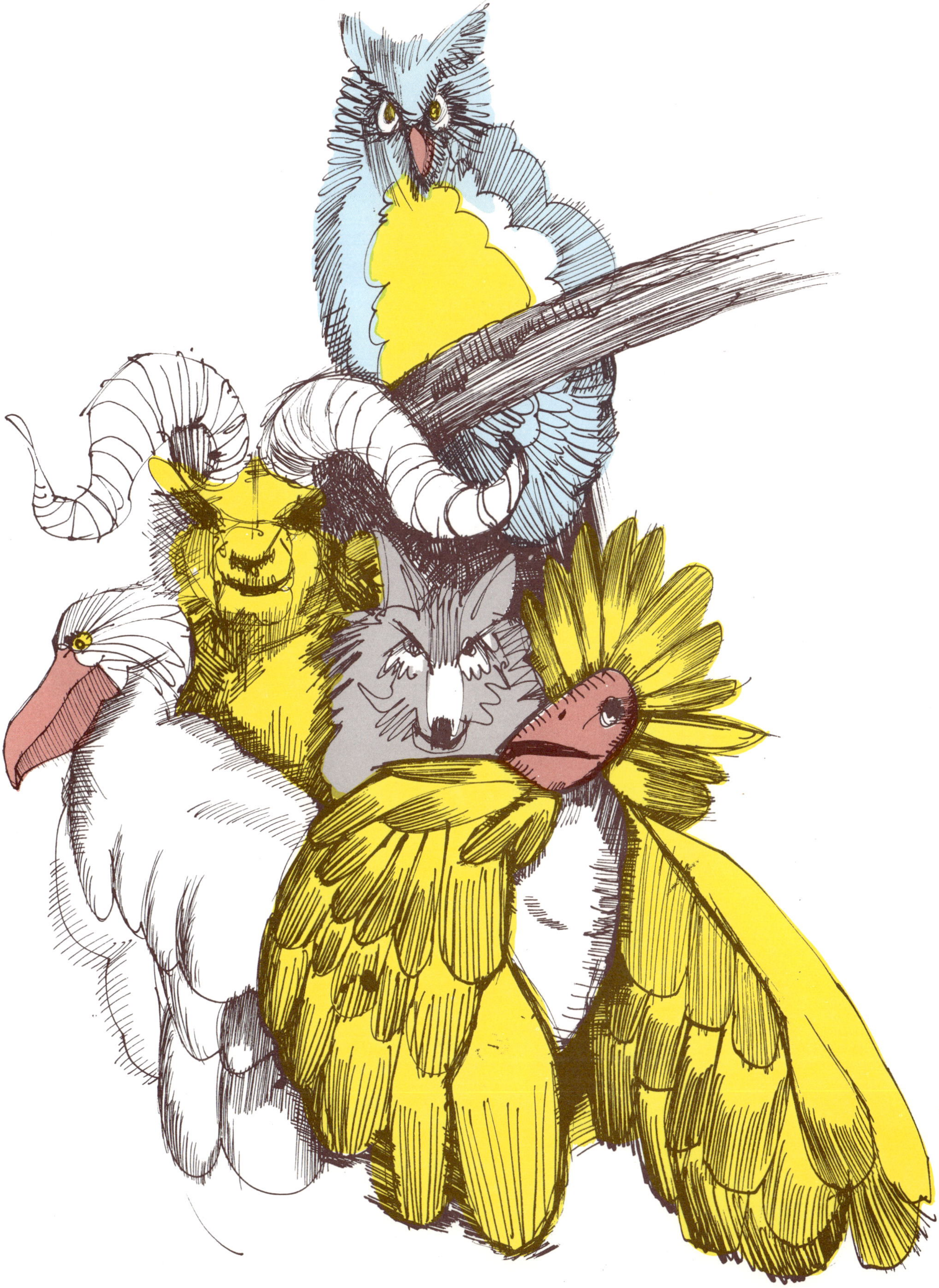

Ifca's Castle

A Round

Czech Folk Song

1. A-bove the val-ley, fresh and green,
2. And seen by day or eve-ning light,

The snow-y peaks are clear-ly seen.
These loft-y peaks give us de-light.

1,2. Rush-ing, rush-ing down be-low, Swift-ly flows the riv - er,

Rush-ing, rush-ing down be-low, Swift-ly flows the riv - er.

Using voices or bells, add these chants. Make up words.

(a) single note

(b)

Rush-ing, rush-ing down be-low.

76

Ah! Poor Bird

A Round

Traditional

Version 1

Ah, poor bird, take thy flight,
Far a-bove the sor-rows of this sad, sad world.

Version 2

Ah, poor bird, take thy flight,
Far a-bove the sor-rows of this sad, sad world.

This song is written in the key of D. The I-chord of this scale is called the D chord.

D-chord

By lowering the middle note of the I-chord a half-step, you can produce a new chord. This is the *D minor* chord. Listen to its sound on the bells or autoharp.

D minor chord

Sing the second version of the melody in the minor key, accompanying yourselves with the *D minor* chord.
Note the different key signatures for the two versions of the song — the first is in the key of D, the second in the key of D minor. When "Ah! Poor Bird" uses the notes of the D minor scale, notice that the seventh note is raised from C to C sharp.

This is called the *harmonic minor scale*.

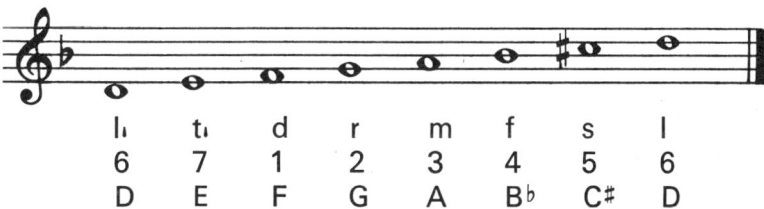

l₁	t₁	d	r	m	f	s	l
6	7	1	2	3	4	5	6
D	E	F	G	A	B♭	C♯	D

77

INTERVAL PREPARATION

d t, l, d   m l t l s   s f m r   l, d l, m l,

Wraggle-Taggle Gipsies, O!

Old English Ballad

1. There were three gyp-sies a-come to my door,
2. Then she pulled off her silk fin-ished gown,

And down-stairs ran this-a la-dy, O!
And down-stairs ran this-a la-dy, O!

The one sang high, and an-oth-er sang low,
The rag-ged rags a—bout— our door,

And the oth-er sang, "Bon-ny, bon-ny Bis-cay, O!"
And she's gone with the wrag-gle-tag-gle gyp-sies, O!"

3. It was late last night when my lord came home,
    Inquiring for his lady, O! The servants said on ev'ry hand,
    "She's gone with the wraggle-taggle gypsies, O!"

The Lord (boys)

4. "O, saddle me my milk-white steed,
    And go and seek my pony, O!
    That I may ride and seek my bride,
    Who is gone with the wraggle-taggle gypsies, O!"

All

5. O, he rode high, and he rode low,
    He rode through woods and copses too
    Until he came to a wide open field,
    And there he espied his a-lady, O!

78

The Lord (*boys*)

6. "What makes you leave your house and land?
   What makes you leave your money, O?
   What makes you leave your new-wedded lord,
   To go with the wraggle-taggle gypsies, O?"

The Lady (*girls*)

7. "What care I for my house and my land?
   And what care I for my money, O?
   What care I for my new-wedded lord?
   I'm off with the wraggle-taggle gypsies, O!"

The Moldau

Smetana

The Moldau (pronounced Moldow) is a large river in Czechoslovakia. The composer, Smetana, wrote a piece for orchestra which describes this river. The main tune of the composition is given above, and is in a minor key. Later in the music this tune is played in the major key. Listen carefully to find it.

The river goes through many changes during the course of the music. *

Listen for these sections:

1. A small rippling mountain stream.
2. The stream is joined by a deeper stream.
3. As they flow together they form the Moldau river (you now hear the tune written above).
4. Through the forest (huntsmen's horns).
5. Through the plains (Village wedding: polka).
6. At night, nymphs play on the waters.
7. Old castles are mirrored in the waters.
8. The rapids of St. John.
9. The river flows majestically past Prague.
10. It disappears in the distance.

* A recording of "The Moldau" is found in *Bowmar Orchestral Library*, No. 60.

INTERVAL PREPARATION

d t, l, s, l,   d t, l, se, l,   l f, t, s, d

Ach Ja!

German Folk Song

When the broth-er and the sis-ter make a vis-it to the fair, Ach ja! Ach ja!
They have-n't an-y mon-ey nor has an-y-bod-y there, Ach ja! Ach ja!
Tra la la, Tra la la, Tra la la la la la la, Tra la la, Tra la la, Tra la la la la la la, Ach ja! Ach ja!

THINGS TO DO Accompany the "Tra la la" chorus on the autoharp or the piano, or both. You will need only the F and C7 chords. Play two chords per bar, one on the first beat and one on the third beat.

Don't forget to give the proper value to each dotted half note.

In your notebook:

1. Write on the bottom space of the treble clef two bars in $\frac{4}{4}$ time using a ♩. note and eighth notes.

DRAMATIZATION

Create a "circle" dance. Improvise your own dance movements appropriate to the music.

MORE ABOUT RHYTHM

Here is the rhythm of water dripping from an eavestrough.

Clap the rhythm. Sing the time names.
Use this rhythm to compose an 8-bar song.
Can you write another familiar rhythm? Listen to your heartbeat, the engine of a motorcycle, the ticking of a watch or clock.

INTERVAL PREPARATION

d l, l, t, d t, l,   l se l   t se l

Drums and Tambourines

In march time

Words by F. Churchley
Music by J. Rameau

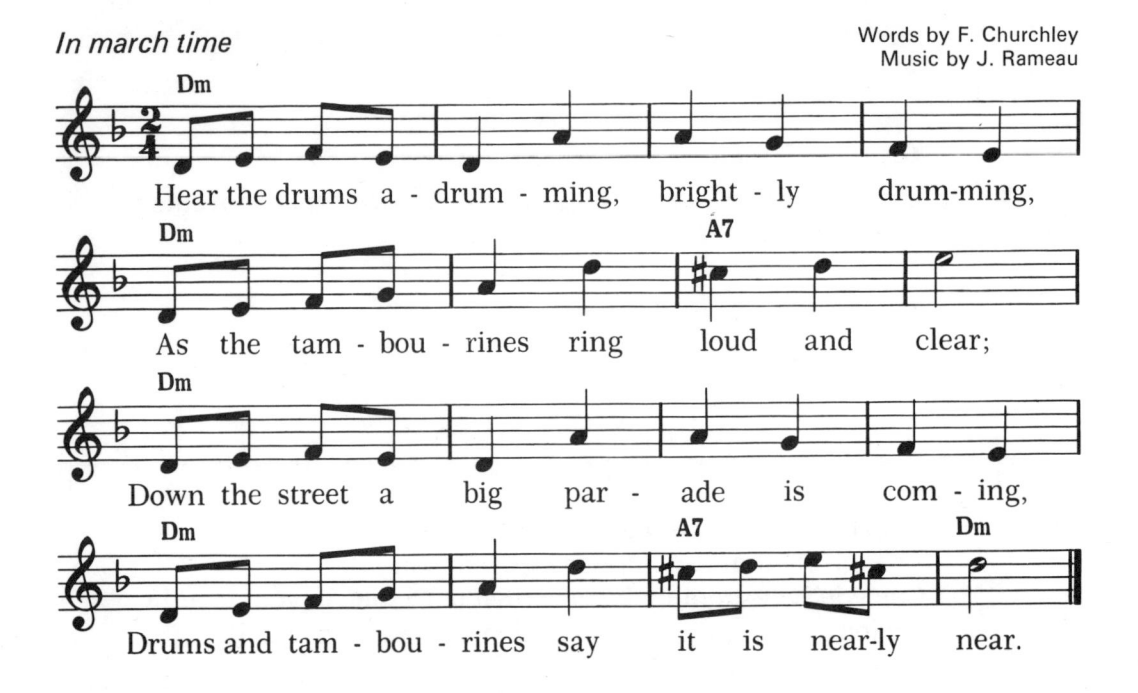

Hear the drums a-drum-ming, bright-ly drum-ming,
As the tam-bou-rines ring loud and clear;
Down the street a big par-ade is com-ing,
Drums and tam-bou-rines say it is near-ly near.

ABOUT THE SONG

The pattern — or, as musicians say, the "form" — of this song is very clear. There are two sections, the first ending in the eighth bar with an unfinished feeling. The second section starts the same way as the first, but changes near the end to make the piece sound complete. Look for repeated patterns in the music. Recognizing them makes music reading much easier.

Notice that composers usually raise (sharpen) the note just below the key note in the minor. In this case all the C's are sharpened (♯). This note is called the *leading note*, since it "leads" your ear back to the key note.

THINGS TO DO

In your notebook, write in the sharpened leading note for these minor key notes.

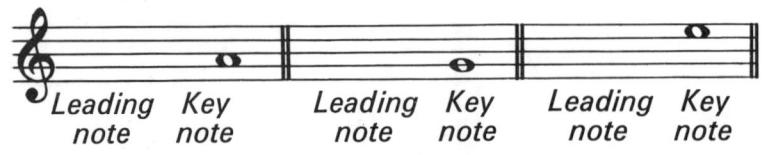

Leading note Key note   Leading note Key note   Leading note Key note

Create a rhythmic accompaniment using drums and tambourines.

Frère Jacques

A Round

Traditional

Melody: (1) Frè-re Jac-ques, Frè-re Jac-ques, (2) Dor-mez-vous? Dor-mez-vous?

Part A: Wake up John! Wake up John! etc.

Part B: Ding dong ding dong etc.

(3) Son-nez les ma-ti-nes, Son-nez les ma-ti-nes, (4) Din din don, Din din don.

THINGS TO DO   Sing this familiar round in French. The accompanying parts A and B can be played first on the piano or bells and then sung.
While one half of the class sings Frère Jacques, the others sing "Three Blind Mice" or "Row, Row, Row Your Boat".
Accompany the song on the autoharp, using the F chord.
For other examples of the soh-doh (5-1) interval, listen to: "Santa Lucia" and "Variations on 'Pop! Goes the Weasel'", both found in *Adventures in Music*. Grade 4, Vol. 1. Both pieces start with this familiar interval.
Find examples of the soh-doh interval in other songs that you have learned.
"Ding Dong" suggests bells. Experiment with all sizes of bells.
Make a set of bells using water glasses.

INTERVAL PREPARATION

s f m f s f m r d t s s d

Streets of Laredo

American Folk Song

As I____ walked out in the streets of La-re-do, As I walked out in La-re-do one day, I spied a poor cow-boy all wrapped in white lin-en, All wrapped in white lin-en as cold as the day.

84

FORM

Other words for *form* are *design* and *pattern*. Just as there is a design in wallpaper, clothing, buildings, automobiles, etc., there is a design or form in music. It is determined by the arrangement of phrases. You have observed, heard, and discussed phrases which are reprinted note for note, phrases which are similar, phrases repeated in sequence, and contrasting phrases which are different to any other phrases in the song. These different kinds of phrases build a pattern which becomes the form of the song.

Form gives music, unity, balance, and variety. It makes music interesting.

ABOUT THE MUSIC

There are four phrases. Find two phrases which are alike. Find two phrases which begin alike but end differently.
The form of this song is A B A C.

THINGS TO DO

Accompany your singing with the autoharp or the piano, using F- and C7-chords.

When you know the tune well, a few students may play the descant part (simply the note C) on the piano or recorder or bells. Then the same group may sing the descant to the syllable "loo", while the rest of the class sings the melody. Then, make up your own words for the descant.

Notice that the note "soh" fits into both the I- and V7-chords.

Conduct the song three beats to the bar

and one beat to the bar.

Which *feels* correct for this song?

85

REVIEW 2

1. Match the world in column A with the right phrase in column B:

A	B
(a) Syncopation	(a) The "home" note
(b) Interval	(b) A group of notes sounded together
(c) Tonic	(c) Plucking stringed instruments
(d) Chord	(d) A set of five notes
(e) Pentatonic scale	(e) A note below the key-note
(f) Leading note	(f) The strong beat comes when you don't expect it
(g) Harpsichord	(g) A keyboard instrument
(h) Pizzicato	(h) The distance between two notes

2. Listen as the teacher plays sets of major, minor, and V7-chords. Name the order in which you hear them.

3. Listen to the teacher play these four phrases on the piano or bells. Write down the order in which they are played.

4. Sing these phrases after the first note has been played on bells, pitch-pipe, or piano:

5. In your notebook, write the following songs, placing bar lines in the proper places.

6. Clap the rhythms. Name the songs from which these rhythms were taken.

INTERVAL PREPARATION

d t l, r r d t, s, l, t, d r d

Voyageur Song

Words by John Murray Gibbon
French-Canadian Folk Song

1. Ho! for the life of a voy-a-geur!
2. Ho! for the tum-bling rap-ids' roar!

Ho! for the haunts of game and fur!
Ho! for the rest on lone lake shore!

We drive a-long the old ca-noe,
We lie be-neath the old ca-noe,

And comb the bank for bea-ver.
And sleep be-side the riv-er.

ABOUT THE MUSIC

A *voyageur* is a traveller. Early travellers in Canada covered thousands of miles by canoe, hunting, fishing, and trapping for food and furs. They sang to relieve the loneliness in the forest and to supply a rhythm to the paddling of their canoes.

Discover scale-wise patterns in the melody.
"Voyageur Song" uses the notes from the scale A♭.

d	r	m	f	s	l	t	d'
1	2	3	4	5	6	7	8
A♭	B♭	C	D♭	E♭	F	G	A♭

87

SHUNIAH SCHOOL

INTERVAL PREPARATION

s, d r f m m r d m f s d r s, l, t, d

Sweet Nightingale

English Folk Song

Pret-ty maid, come a - long! Don't you hear the sweet song, The sweet notes of the night - in - gale flow? — Don't you hear the fond tale of the sweet night - in - gale, As he sings in the val - ley be - low? —————— As he sings in the val - ley be - low? ——

What kind of tone suits this song?
Conduct and *feel* one beat to the bar so the singing will flow.
Try singing phrase 3 and phrase 4 in one long breath.

Slumber Song

Words by Grace Budd
Melody by Franz Schubert

1. Sleep thou! ba - by mine, In thy cra—dle— rock - ing;
   Soft wings pause and shine 'Round thy pil—low— white.
   Hush! While thy moth - er sings Songs of—old - en fan - cy;
   Morn drops down from God, On the creep—ing— night.

2. Low to thee, my dear! Bends thy moth—er— hum - ming;
   Stars shine sil - ver, dear! In the dusk—y— sky.
   Fears shall not mar thy sleep; No sound—shall a - wake thee;
   Sleep, my ba - by sleep; Till the dark—creeps— by.

Listen to this song on RCA Victor Listening Program for Primary Grades, Volume I.

What kind of tone will you use for this song?
Suggest a tempo for this song. Find phrases which are alike.
Find phrases which are similar.

ABOUT THE COMPOSER

Franz Schubert, born in Vienna, Austria, in 1797, was a master of writing beautiful melodies. He composed over 600 songs during his short life of thirty-one years. His genius in creating melody has rarely been matched.

Listen also to Schubert's "Marche Militaire" (Bowmar Orchestral Library No. 54).

Heigh Ho, Anybody Home?

English Folk Song

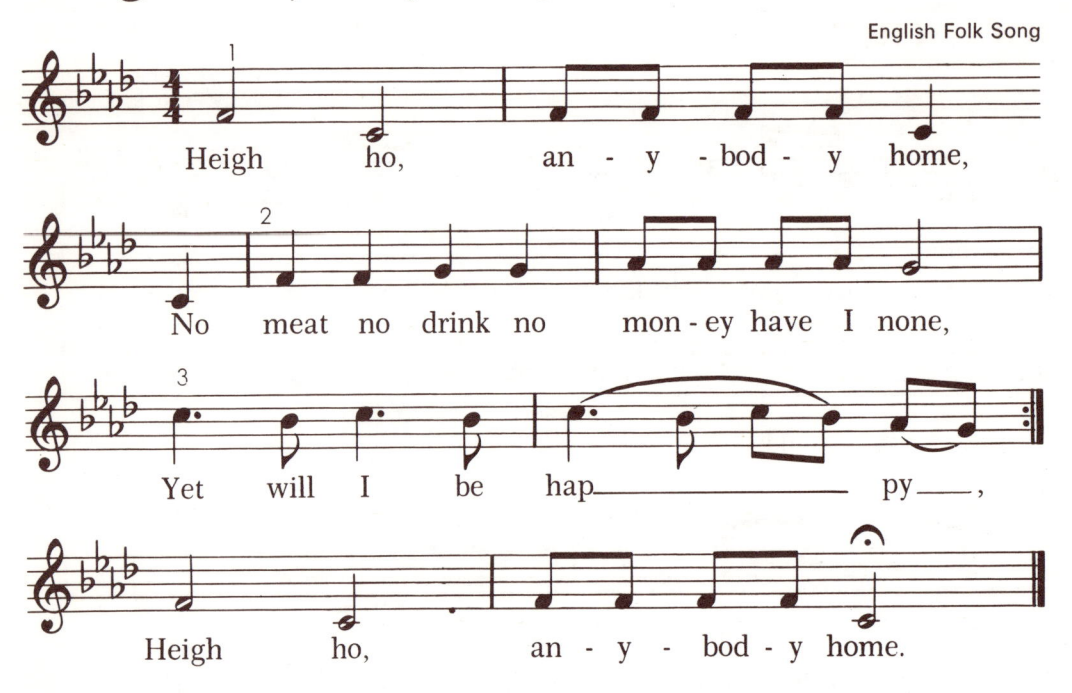

Heigh ho, an-y-bod-y home,
No meat no drink no mon-ey have I none,
Yet will I be hap_____py___,
Heigh ho, an-y-bod-y home.

ABOUT THE MUSIC

This song is in the key of F minor.

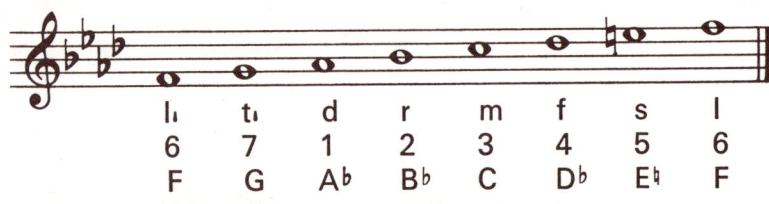

l,	t,	d	r	m	f	s	l
6	7	1	2	3	4	5	6
F	G	A♭	B♭	C	D♭	E♭	F

The symbol ⌒ means hold the note appearing under it.
Is there a leading note in this song?
If there were a leading note, what would it be?
This round starts with the familiar interval of a 4th, from doh to soh. Sing it! You can accompany this piece by playing the F *minor* chord at the beginning of each bar.

F minor 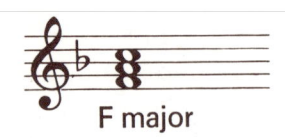   F major

"Heigh Ho, Anybody Home?" is an example of minor music that is gay and happy. At what bar are you sure the song is in a minor key?

THINGS TO DO

Try this song in the major key by changing the A♭ note to A. Which do you prefer?

Use the first or last bar as a chant, singing "Heigh-ho" or "Anybody home".

In your notebook:

1. Write the notes one-half step lower than each of the following:

   Play these notes on the piano or bells.

2. Write (a) the G minor chord.
   (b) the D minor chord.

3. Sing or play these chords on the piano or bells.

Czech Dance

Translation by N. Hesky and N. Adaskin

Boys are lea-ping jum-ping high, Girls are clap-ping, "Hey!" they cry.

He who jumps the high-est wins, Girls will call "Our dance be-gins!"

2. Who will take the goats to town?
   I will take them down, down, down.
   I would lead them with no fear,
   If the wolf were never near.

Playing the Recorder

The recorder has been a popular instrument for many centuries. It is now being used widely in school classes because it is not a difficult instrument to play. Once you have mastered it, there are many fine instrumental pieces you will be able to play. You will find, also, that it will help you in learning new songs and reading music. Begin by covering the first three holes and the under-side hole of your recorder with the first three fingers and thumb of the left hand, thus:

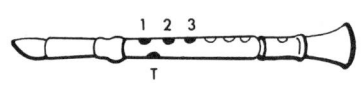

This is note G:

Before playing note G, be sure your thumb and first three fingers are completely covering the holes; try to keep your fingers relaxed. Shape your lips over the mouthpiece as if you were saying *too* or *doo*. Blow steadily and easily as you practise the following:

For note A, raise the 3rd finger to uncover the hole.

Repeat the exercise above, this time on A. For note B  raise also the 2nd finger, leaving only two holes covered. Repeat the exercise, this time on B.

Note A: Note B:

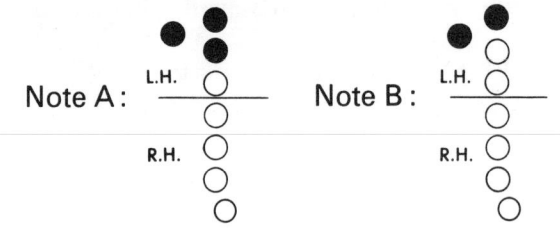

You are now ready to play your first melody. (Don't forget to let the breath out easily and steadily.)

EXERCISE I

EXERCISE II

EXERCISE III

Here is part of a melody you sang on page 52. (Don't forget to shape *too* and *doo* with your lips, so that the sound is crisp and bright.)

HARMONY

Play the C chord on the autoharp. (A chord is named for the note on which it is built.) The C chord is also known as the I-chord, the tonic chord (because I is the tonic), the home chord, or the doh chord. C is called the root, the tonic, the home tone, or doh. The C chord has three tones and looks like this on the staff.

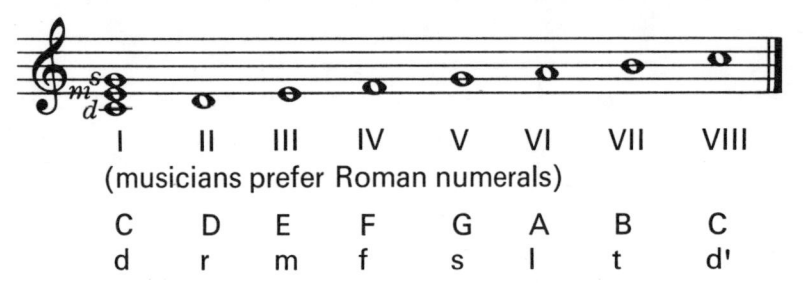

I	II	III	IV	V	VI	VII	VIII

(musicians prefer Roman numerals)

C	D	E	F	G	A	B	C
d	r	m	f	s	l	t	d'

Many songs can be accompanied by the I-chord. The second most important chord is built on the fifth step or degree of the scale. It is known as the dominant or V-chord. In the scale of C it is built on G and would be known as the G chord.

I	II	III	IV	V	VI	VII	VIII

By adding a fourth note or tone, F, to the dominant chord, we get a richer sound.

The new chord is called the dominant seventh (dominant because it is built on the fifth or dominant degree of the scale, and seventh because the new note added, D, is the seventh note on the scale). The dominant seventh, usually called V7, looks like this:

I	II	III	IV	V	VI	VII	VIII

Listen to I and V7 in various keys using the autoharp, piano, or bells. Can you hear the difference between these two chords? V7 is a restless chord. It is not a chord to conclude a song. Most songs end with these chords in this manner: V7 to I.

The third most important chord is built on the fourth tone of the scale.

Listen to and compare the sounds of I — IV — V7 in the key of C, G, F.

Here is the IV chord:

I	II	III	IV	V	VI	VII	VIII
C	D	E	F	G	A	B	C
d	r	m	f	s	l	t	d'

Auld Lang Syne

Scottish Folk Song

Should auld ac-quaint-ance be for-got and nev-er brought to mind, Should auld acquaintance be for-got and days of Auld Lang Syne.

THINGS TO DO

Like many Scottish songs, this melody is *pentatonic*. It can be played on the black keys of the piano starting on F sharp. It can also be played on the bells.

Sing the melody to syllables.
Sing the words as you accompany your singing with bells.

Which ostinato * do you prefer — bar 5 or bars 7 and 8 ? Use bells, or voices, or both.

Bar 5   Bars 7 and 8

An ostinato is a melodic pattern that can be repeated to accompany a melody.

Kookaburra

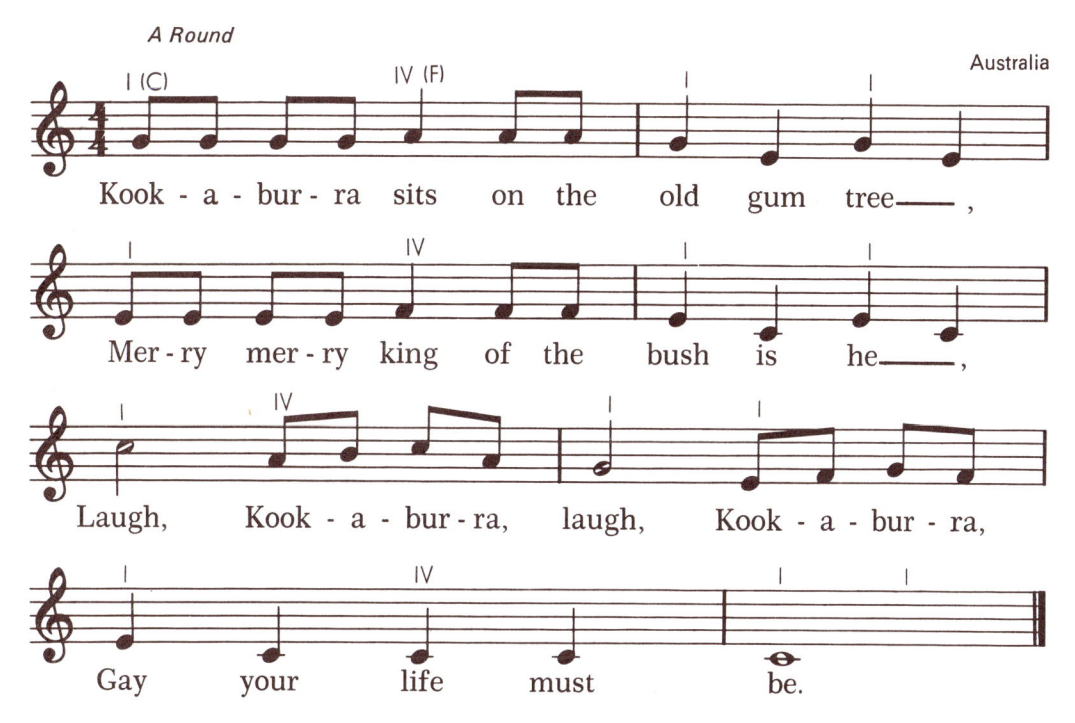

A Round

Australia

Kook-a-bur-ra sits on the old gum tree—,
Mer-ry mer-ry king of the bush is he—,
Laugh, Kook-a-bur-ra, laugh, Kook-a-bur-ra,
Gay your life must be.

Accompany your singing on the autoharp, using the C and F chords.

Listen to the other parts as you sing.

When you sing "Kookaburra" as a round, the second group enters at bar 3.

O How Lovely Is the Evening

A Round

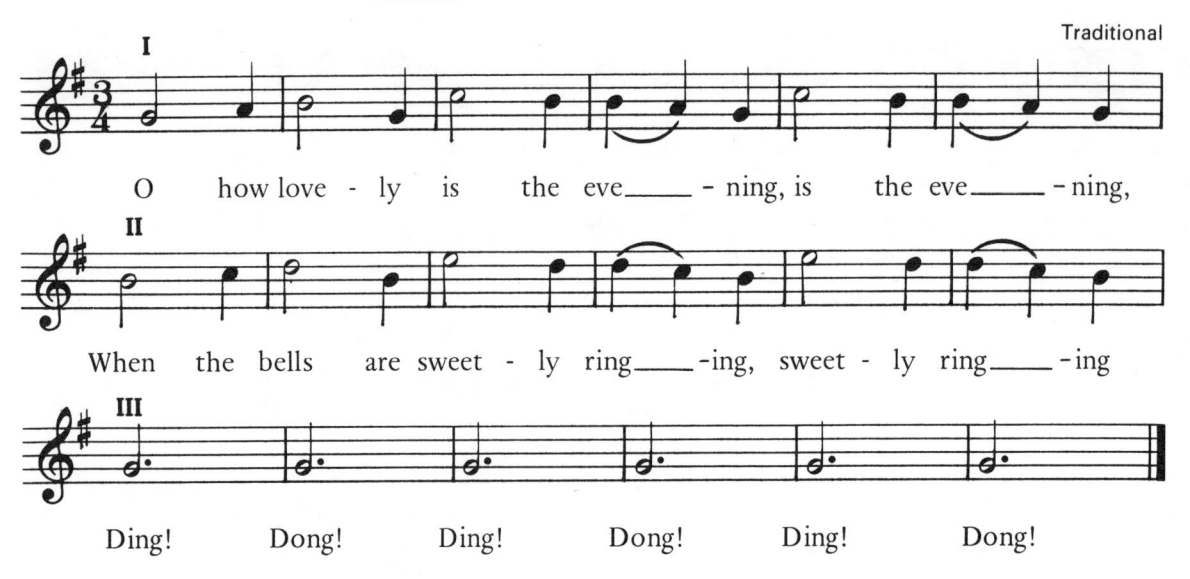

Traditional

I

O how love-ly is the eve——-ning, is the eve——-ning,

II

When the bells are sweet-ly ring——-ing, sweet-ly ring——-ing

III

Ding! Dong! Ding! Dong! Ding! Dong!

THINGS TO DO

This round needs the same two chords as Kookaburra: the I-chord and the IV-chord.

Begin accompanying this round with the I-chord. Let your ears tell you when you need to use the IV-chord and when you should return to the I-chord.

When you have decided on the order of chords that sounds best, write the chord pattern in your notebook.

For your recorder:

Notice the new note E and its fingering. You will need to use your right hand fingers as well.

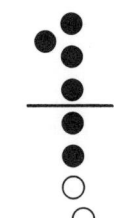

Note E

Note C is found by covering the 2nd hole and thumb hole thus:

For note D remove the thumb, leaving only the 2nd hole covered.

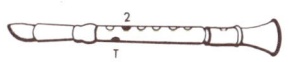

Review notes G, A, and B, and then play the following tune, an old Norwegian dance:

Fine

EDVARD GRIEG

Edvard Grieg was born in Norway. Although he studied in Germany, he went back to Norway and became one of his country's most famous composers. He loved the Norwegian folk tunes, and much of his music is based on them.

"In the Hall of the Mountain King" is an orchestra piece from Peer Gynt Suite No. I. Peer Gynt was a gay young man whose adventures are in Grieg's music. You will find his complete story in *Music for Young Listeners: The Crimson Book*, by Lillian Baldwin. In this part of the story, he meets the king of the trolls, who are very much like goblins. The main tune is in the minor key and sounds very mysterious on the low stringed instruments played *pizzicato*.

Follow this tune as you listen to the music. It is recorded in *Adventures in Music*, Grade 3, Vol. 2, and in *Bowmar Orchestral Library*, No. 59.

THINGS TO DO You can play this theme from "Ase's Death", part of Grieg's "Peer Gynt Suite No. 1" on your recorders.

Peer Gynt Suite Theme

Edvard Grieg

Play the song below by Grieg on your recorders. Notice the new note to finger:

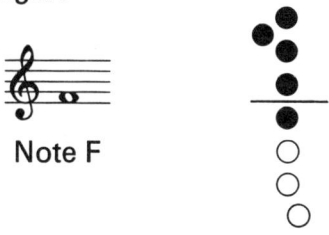

Note F

My Homeland

Music by Edvard Grieg
Words by Joan Field

O - ver the sea, my home-land, to where my life be - gan,

Soon I shall see the moun-tains, the val-leys and the plains.

Both of the tunes on this page are in minor keys. Can you tell why?

Way Up on the Mountain

Savoie Folk Song

Way up on the high moun-tain, there was an old cha - let.

Way up on the high moun-tain, there was an old cha - let.

The snow and rocks to - geth - er came and car - ried it a - way.

Way up on the high moun-tain, there was an old cha - let.

2. Way up on the high mountain,
   There is a new chalet,
   For John went up with logs
   And built another, nicer still!
   Way up on the high mountain,
   There is a new chalet.

ABOUT THE MUSIC

What is the letter name of the first note in the song?
What is the letter name of the second note in the song?
Because these two notes have the same name and are eight notes apart (counting the bottom note as the first) they are said to be the interval of an *octave* apart.

Discover phrases which are alike.
Find the octave jump.

Taking turns at the piano or the bells, play these notes, following each by the note an octave higher.
Write octave notes for each of these notes in your notebook.

Sing the notes you have written.

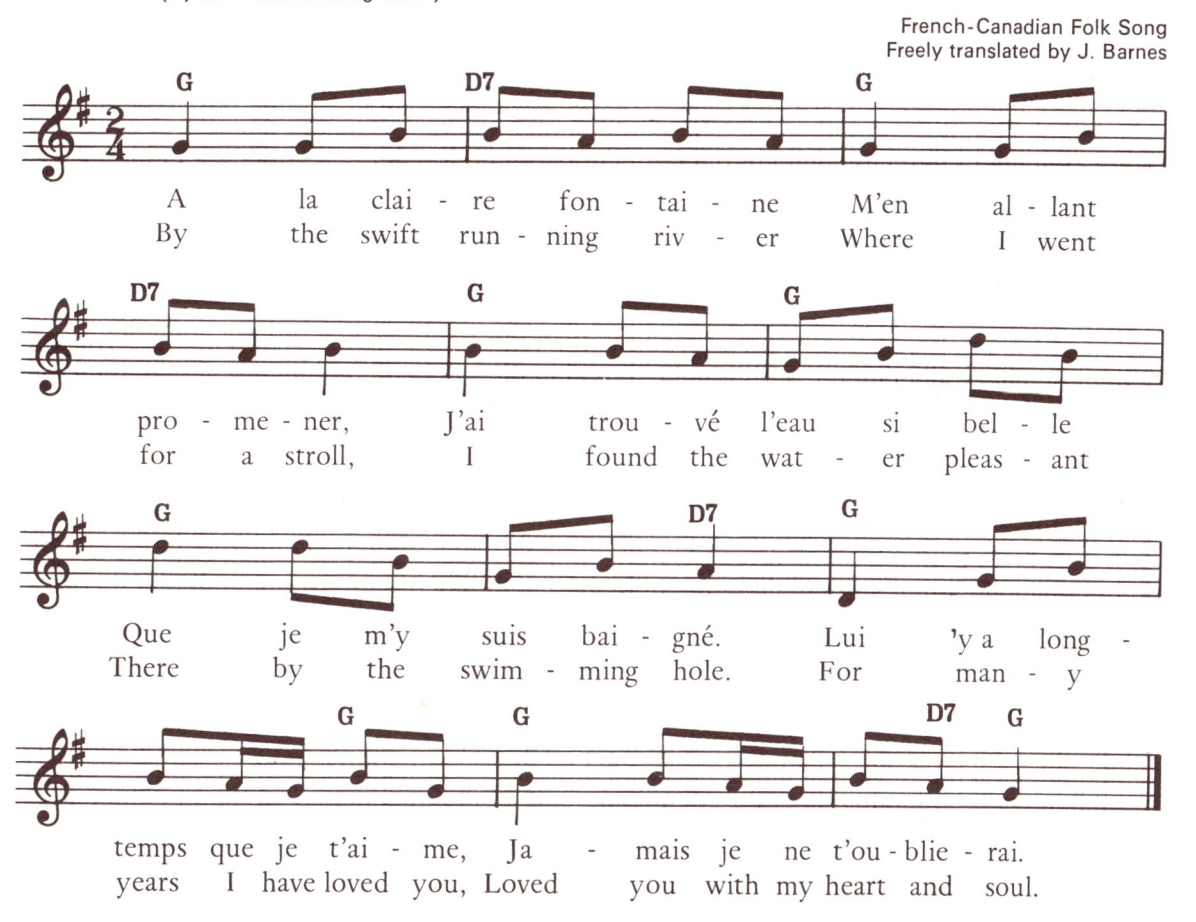

A la Claire Fontaine
(By the Swift Running River)

French-Canadian Folk Song
Freely translated by J. Barnes

A la clai - re fon - tai - ne M'en al - lant pro - me - ner, J'ai trou - vé l'eau si bel - le Que je m'y suis bai - gné. Lui 'y a long - temps que je t'ai - me, Ja - mais je ne t'ou - blie - rai.

By the swift run - ning riv - er Where I went for a stroll, I found the wat - er pleas - ant There by the swim - ming hole. For man - y years I have loved you, Loved you with my heart and soul.

Listen to a recording of French-Canadian folk songs such as "Mon Canada", recorded by the Montreal Bach Choir. "A La Claire Fontaine" is included.

Night Herding Song

Cowboy Song

Go slow, lit-tle do-gies, stop mil-ling a-round, For I'm tired of your rov-ing all o-ver the ground. There's grass where you're stand-ing, so feed kind of slow, And you don't have for-e-ver to be on the go. Move slow, lit-tle do-gies move slow. Hi-o, hi-o, hi-o.

2. Lay down, little dogies, and when you've laid down,
   You can stretch yourselves out, for there's plenty of ground.
   Stay put, little dogies, for I'm awful tired,
   And if you get away I am sure to be fired,
   Lay down, little dogies, lay down. Hio, hio, hio.

THINGS TO DO

Suggest the tempo for this song.
Accompany this song with the two most common chords, I and V7. In the key of F, these two chords are called F and C7 chords. Both the autoharp and the piano would be suitable for this piece.
Can you find an example of the interval of an octave in this piece?
For variety, substitute the G minor (Gm) chord for the C7-chord on the autoharp.
Write out two rhythm patterns found in this song.

MUSIC FOR LISTENING

"On the Trail", by Grofé; *Bowmar Orchestral Library*, No. 61.
Songs of the West, Norman Luboff choir.

Signs of Spring

GRASS

Grass
Cooling, sponging, tickling
Makes my feet feel Spring.

Paul Knowles

PUSSY WILLOW

Soft, furry kittens
Suspended on a branch,
Shed their brown shelters
And show their beauty to the
spring-promised world.

Aroka Cameron
Grade Five

COLOURFUL SPRING

Grass green,
Crocus yellow,
Tulip red,
Sun golden,
Sky blue.

Margot Caldwell

WHAT IS SPRING

A new time
A quiet time,
A special time
Of feeling.
A soft time
A soothing time
When life is at
Its beginning.

By Rosemary Burd
Grade Five

SPRING

Cloven hooves
Run through the forest,
The bearded one
Blows his pipe again.

Carolyn Chesney
Grade Five

BUDS

Tiny brown humps
Fill with the liquid of life.

Stephen Walton
Grade Five

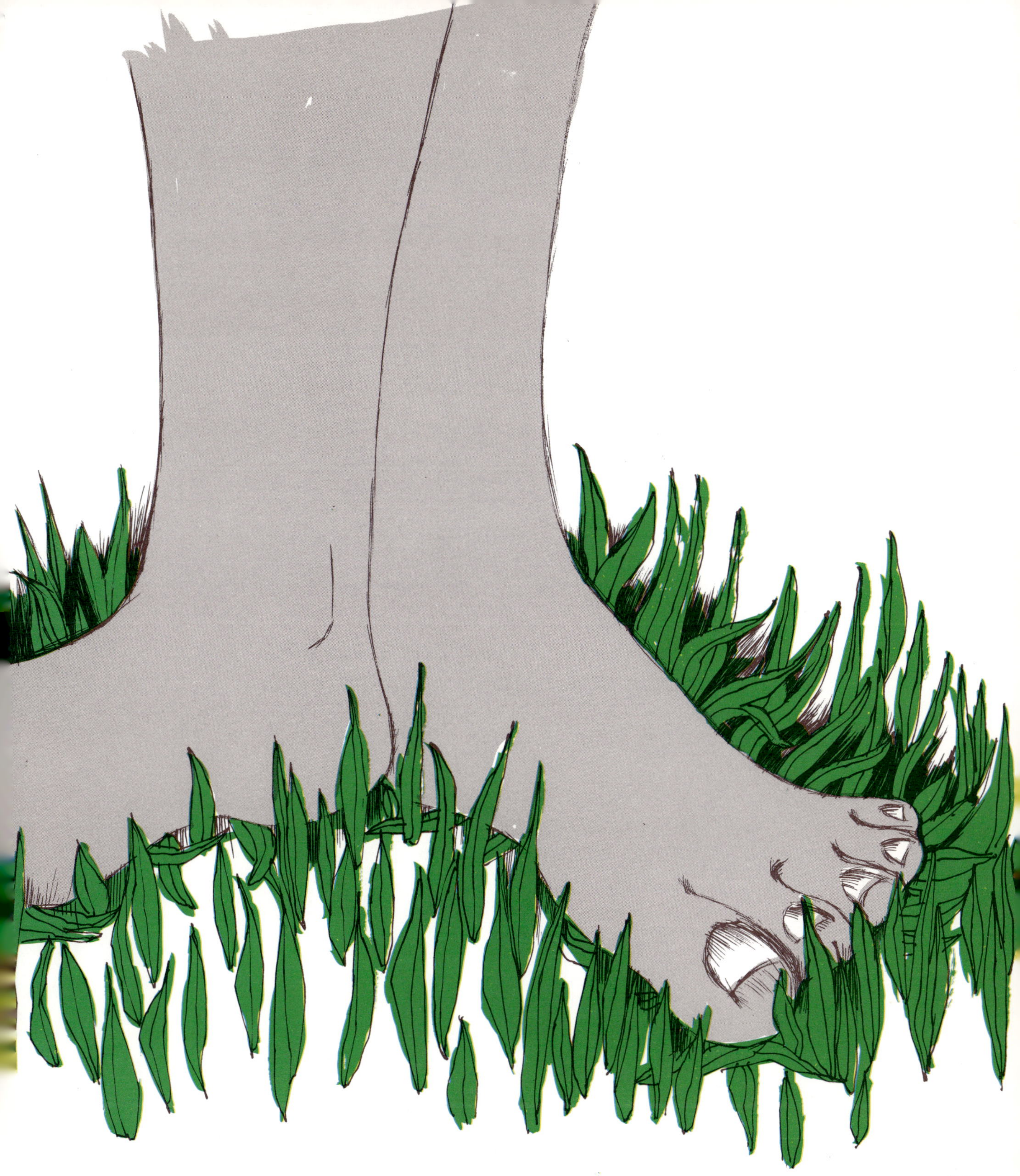

Easter Hymn

Cyril Mossop

Hail this hap-py Eas-ter-time!
Ring the bells and play— the chime!
We shall sing in this— glad hour,
"Christ the Lord hath shown— his power.
Al-le-lu - - ia———!"

    2. Now the flow'rs spring through the ground,
       Hark, the birds sing with a glad sound.
       All the earth bursts forth with life,
       Christ has triumphed over strife. Alleluia!

    3. Trumpets blow majestic sound,
       Bells peal forth their merry round,
       Sin and death Christ doth destroy,
       Easter is a time for joy. Alleluia!

Spring

During this season the air is filled with the music of the birds. Here are two rounds which suggest their joyful sounds. The Hungarian round may be sung in eighteen parts and the Icelandic round in four parts. The next voice enters when the first voice reaches the *.

Spring Round

Hungary

Swal - low, cuc - koo, swift draw near, through the sky come fly - ing Tell us that the Spring is here And that Win - ter's dy - ing Build your nests, be - gin to sing, Let your wood-land voi - ces ring spring is here a - gain!

On the Moor

Iceland

On the moor there lives a plo - ver, And a cur - lew flies high o - ver, 'Pee - wit, pee - wit,' Spring has sure - ly come once more.

Cornish May Song

17th Century English Morris Dance
Words by Sir Alexander Boswell

Ye country maidens, gather dew,
The cobweb rings are fresh and new,
While yet the morning breezes blow,
Do not disturb them as you go.

CHORUS

Arise, arise, the night is past,
Care get thee hence, from this place fly,
The skylark hails the dawn of day,
For mirth rules here this morn of May.

What is the mood of this song?
What kind of tone will convey the spirit of the music?

REVIEW 3

1. Are the following statements true or false?
   (a) Edvard Grieg was born in Germany.
   (b) The symbol ⌒ placed over a note means that the note should be held longer.
   (c) An octave is an interval of the fifth.
   (d) Syncopation means the strong beat is where you would expect it.

2. Listen as the teacher plays I, IV, and V7 chords. Name the order in which you hear them.

3. What are the names of the following intervals? (Remember to count the bottom note as the first.)

   (a)    (b)    (c)    (d)

4. Write the time signature for each of these rhythm patterns:

   Example: 2/4 ♩ ♫ ♩ | ♫ ♫ ♩ |

   (a) 
   (b) 
   (c) 
   (d)

111

Who Has Seen the Wind?

Christina Rossetti
Music by Earle Terry

Who has seen the wind? Nei-ther you nor I,
But when the leaves hang tremb-ling The wind is pas-sing by.
Who has seen the wind? Nei-ther you nor I.
But when the trees bow down their heads The wind is pas-sing by.

Haru Ga Kita

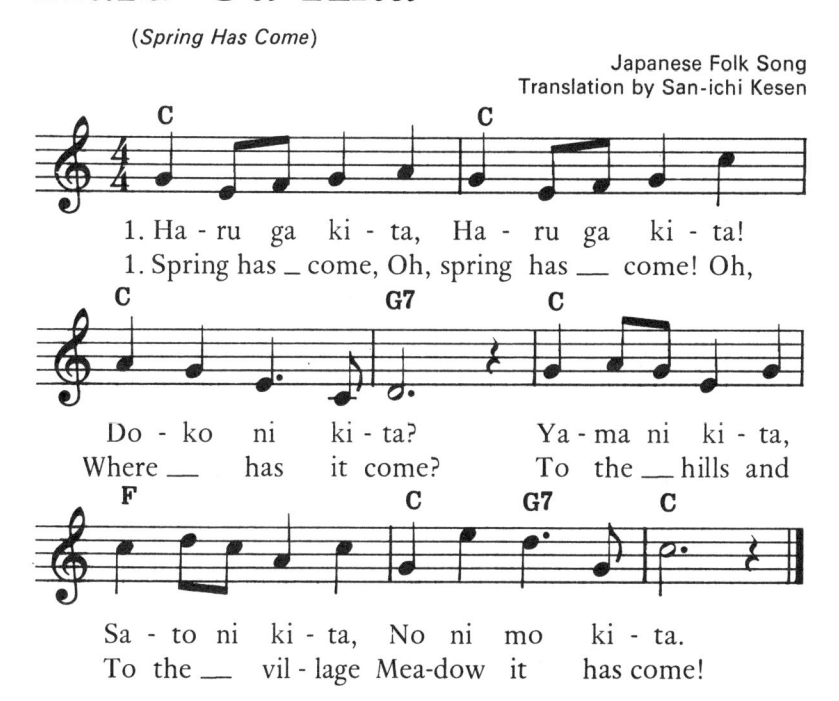

(Spring Has Come)

Japanese Folk Song
Translation by San-ichi Kesen

1. Ha - ru ga ki - ta, Ha - ru ga ki - ta!
1. Spring has come, Oh, spring has come! Oh,

Do - ko ni ki - ta? Ya - ma ni ki - ta,
Where has it come? To the hills and

Sa - to ni ki - ta, No ni mo ki - ta.
To the vil - lage Mea-dow it has come!

2. Hana ga saku,   2. Flowers are blooming,
   Hana ga saku!   Flowers are blooming!
   Doko ni saku?   Where do they bloom?
   Yama ni saku,   On the hills and
   Sato ni saku,   On the village
   No ni mo saku.   Meadow see them bloom!

A favourite spring song of Japanese children.

Learn and sing the Japanese text, keeping in mind the English translation of each of the following words.

haru — spring
kita — come
doko — where
yama — hills or mountain
sato — village
no — meadow or plain

Land of the Silver Birch

Rhythmically

Ontario Folk Song

Land of the sil-ver birch, home of the bea-ver,

Where still the might-y moose wan-ders at will;

Blue lake and rock-y shore, I will re-turn once more.

Boom de de boom boom, Boom de de boom boom

Boom de de boom boom boom.

*Accompaniment repeats throughout. Use piano, xylophone, or bells for accompaniment.

2. High on a rocky ledge I'll build my wigwam,
Close by the water's edge silent and still;
Blue lake and rocky shore, I will return once more.
Boom de de boom, etc.

114

ABOUT THE MUSIC

Boys and girls in summer camps in Northern Ontario have sung this song as a favourite for many years.

Name the song where this rhythm appears:

Use the rhythm below as a chant for voice or drum.

Find other pentatonic songs in your book.

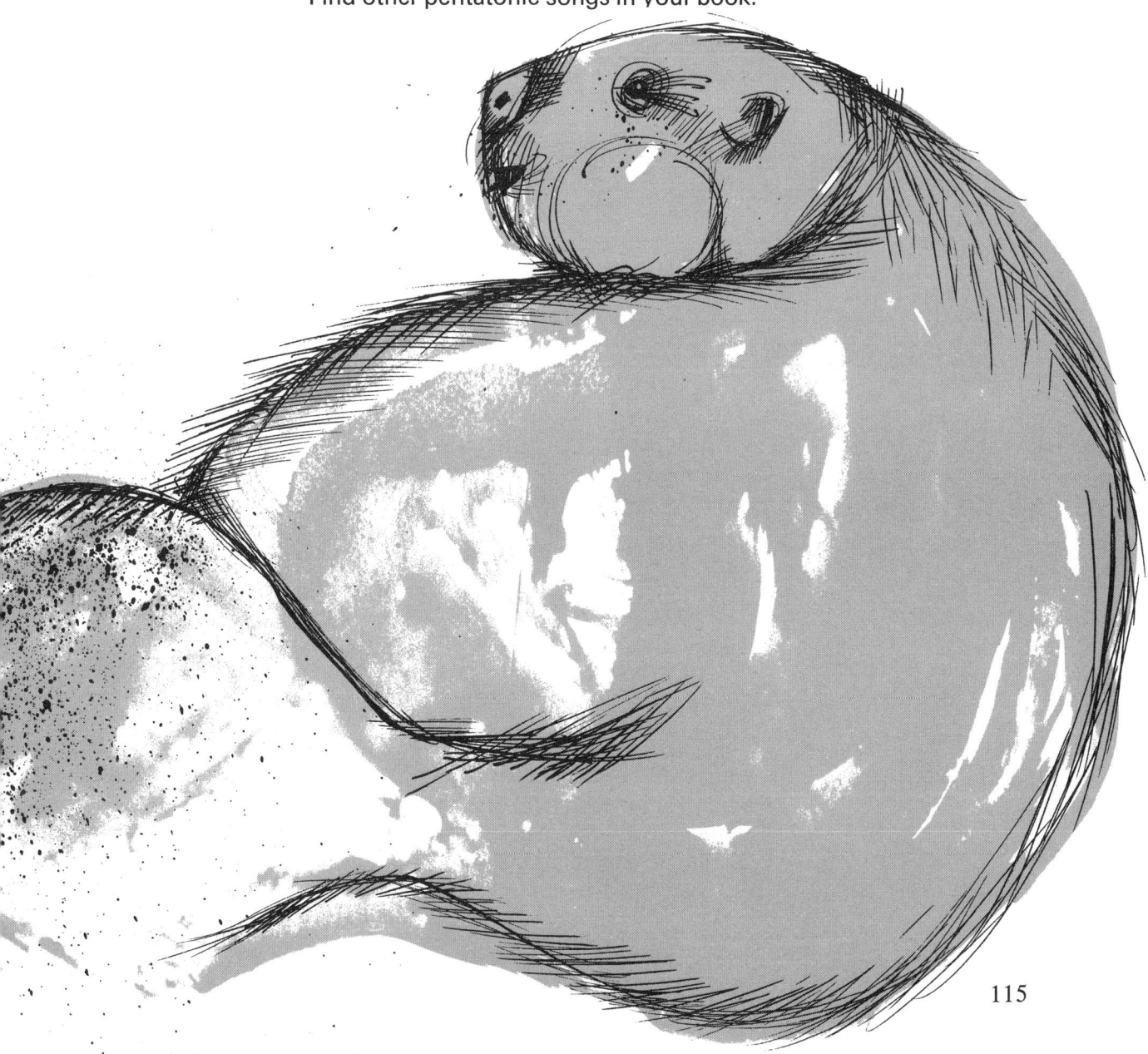

En Roulant, Ma Boule

Lively

French-Canadian Folk Song

En rou-lant ma bou-le rou-lant, En rou-lant ma bou——-le,

Der-rièr' chez nous, ya-t-un é-tang, En rou-lant ma
Be-hind our house we have a pond, Roll on, rol-ling

bou-le, Trois beaux ca-nards s'en vont bai-gnant, Rou-
ball,—— Where three fine ducks swim round and round, Roll

li, rou-lant, ma bou-le rou-lant, En rou-lant ma
on, roll on, my ball—— roll on; On, roll on, my

bou-le rou-lant, En rou-lant ma bou—— -le.
ball—— roll on, On, roll on, my rol-ling ball!

Conduct two beats to the bar.

ABOUT THE MUSIC   In this lively French song, a favourite paddling song of early voyageurs, the music rolls along like the rolling ball in the words. How many times are the first three notes repeated in the music? Call them 3-2-1 (or me-re-doh) and play them on the bells, piano, or recorders each time they occur in the music.

THINGS TO DO In your notebook, write the notes 3-2-1 (me-re-doh) in the keys of C, G, and F (in whole notes).
Mystery Tune: Can you name this familiar nursery rhyme tune?

FOR YOUR RECORDER To play this song on your recorder, you will need the fingering for F♯:

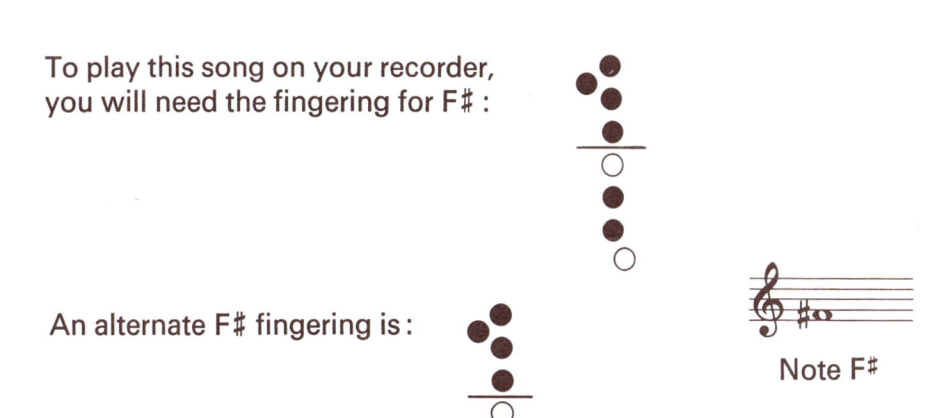

An alternate F♯ fingering is:

Note F♯

Choose the fingering which sounds best on your recorder.

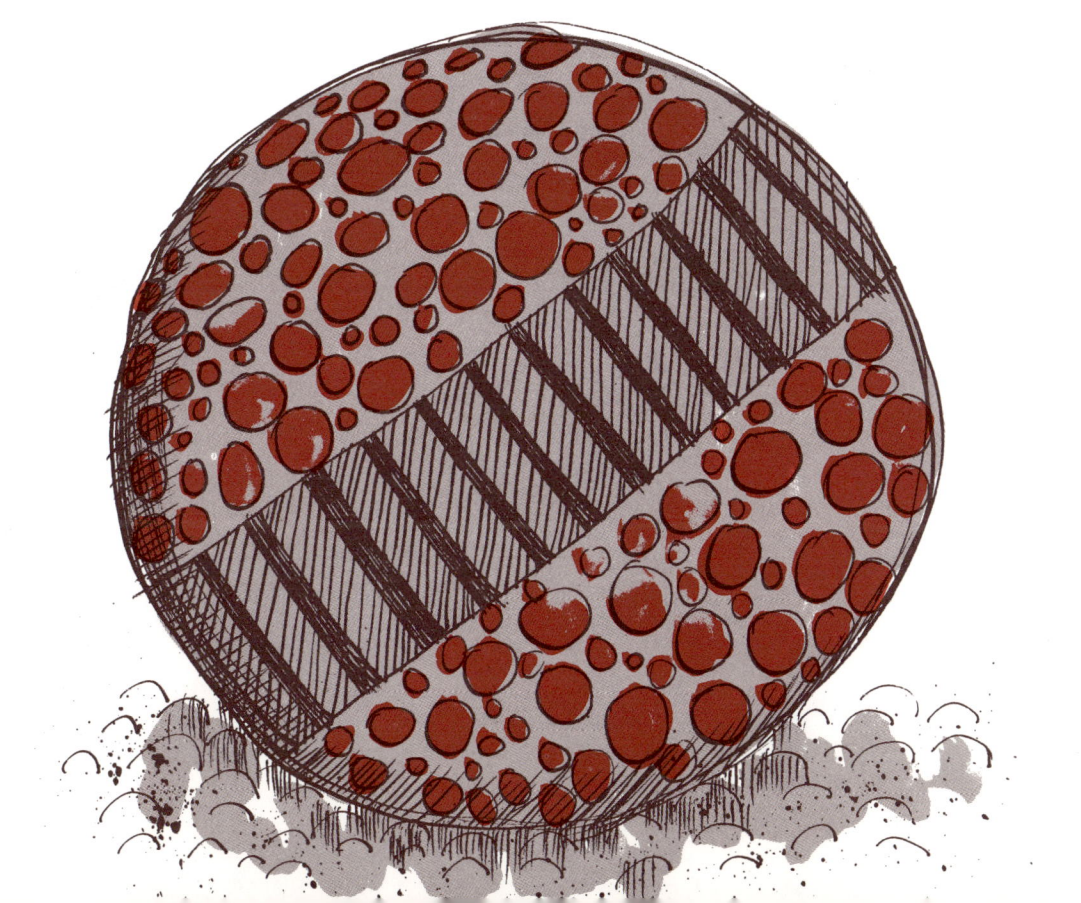

The Snoring Man

French Folk Song
Words by David Warrack

There was a man in Can - a - da*, was known for be - ing la - zy; He slept in late, made busi - ness wait, he thought that it was cra - zy! He liked to snore, Oh what a bore; Oh what a roar when he slept more; He liked to snore, Oh what a bore; Oh what a roar when he slept more, roar! roar!

* Substitute here the name of your school or your town.

118

ABOUT
THE SONG

The tune of this old French song is several hundred years old. The original words were written at the time of the Emperor Napoleon, making fun of him. The new English words are in the same lighthearted mood.

What are the names of the only four notes used in the first three lines of the music?

THINGS TO DO

Sing the song through once. Now play it, using recorders for the first half and bells for the second half.

Compare the last pair of lines of music with the next to last pair. Two things make them easy to read:

1. The last two lines are almost exactly like the two just before them. (What is the only difference?)

2. The groups of four notes in the brackets ⌐──┐ are very much alike, except that the whole pattern of notes is moved down a step. Patterns of notes that are the same, except that they are moved down or up, are called *sequences*.

Look for sequences in the songs "Amsterdam", "Frère Jacques", "Ah Poor Bird", and "Sweet Nightingale".

Can't You Dance the Polka?

Vigorously
Sea Shanty

As I came down the bow-'ry one eve-ning in Ju-ly,
I met a maid who asked my trade and "A sail-or boy," said I.
Then a-way, you san-ty! My dear An-nie,
Oh, you cit-y girls, can't you dance the pol-ka?

2. To Tiffany's I took her,   I bought her two gold earrings,
    I did not mind expense,   They cost me fifty cents.

Originally a shore ballad with the title "Larry Doolan", this song has become familiar as a sea shanty with the sailors' words given here.

The music uses the three common chords: I, IV, and V7. In the key of C, these chords are named C, F, and G7.

Add as many instruments as you can to make the piece interesting. Later, the bells or recorder part can be sung to the words "Dance the Polka". What pattern do you recognize in these four notes?

Doon the Moor

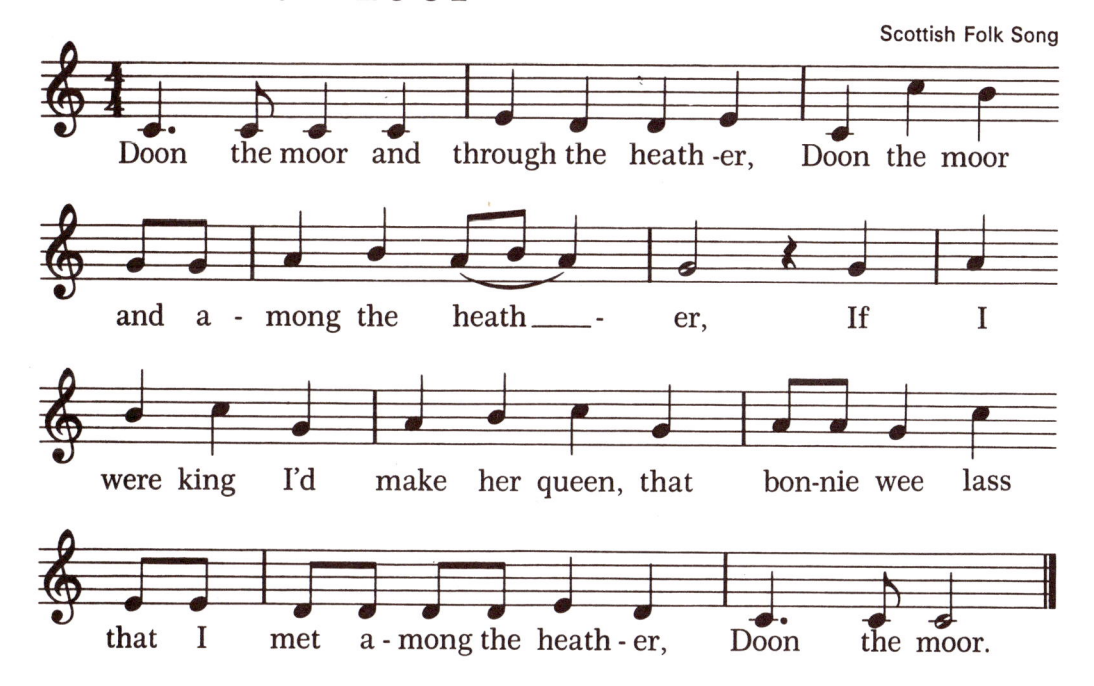

Scottish Folk Song

Doon the moor and through the heath-er, Doon the moor and a-mong the heath—er, If I were king I'd make her queen, that bon-nie wee lass that I met a-mong the heath-er, Doon the moor.

This is a song from Scotland. "Doon the moor" is the way a Scot would say "down the meadows".

In the song, find examples of:

1. A dotted rhythm (like "Amsterdam");
2. An octave jump.

Bonhomme! Bonhomme!

Rollicking
French-Canadian Folk Song

Bon-homm' bon-homm' sais-tu jou-er? Bon-homm' bon-homm' sais-tu jou-er? Sais-tu jou-er de ce vi-o-lon-là? Sais-tu jou-er de ce vi-o-lon-là? Zing zing zing de ce vi-o-lon-là, Bon-homm'———! Tu n'es pas maîtr' dans ta mai-son quand nous y som-mes———!

Bud-dy bud-dy do you play this? Bud-dy bud-dy do you play this? Do you play this on your vi-o-lin? Do you play this on your vi-o-lin? Zing zing zing on your vi-o-lin, Bud-dy———! You aren't the boss in your own house when we are play-ing———!

2. Sais-tu jouer de cett' flûte-là?
   Flût, flût, flût, de cett' flûte-là.

3. Sais-tu jouer de ce tambour-là?
   Boom de boom de ce tambour-là.

2. Do you play on the recorder?
   Tootle toot on the recorder.

3. Do you play on the big brass drum?
   Boom, boom boom on the big brass drum.

ABOUT THE SONG This is another cumulative song (like "We are Musicians"). Remember, this means that you repeat all instruments each time one is added. For example, after chorus 3 ("Boom de boom de ce tambour-là"), sing chorus 2 ("Flût, flût, flût, de cett' flûte-là"), then chorus 1 ("Zing, zing, zing," etc.)

THINGS TO DO

1. Try singing the French words and imitating the actions of the various instruments. Use real instruments when they are available. The recorder, for example, might play the line "Flût, flût, flût, de cett' flûte-là".

2. In your notebook write the following patterns several times in sequence:

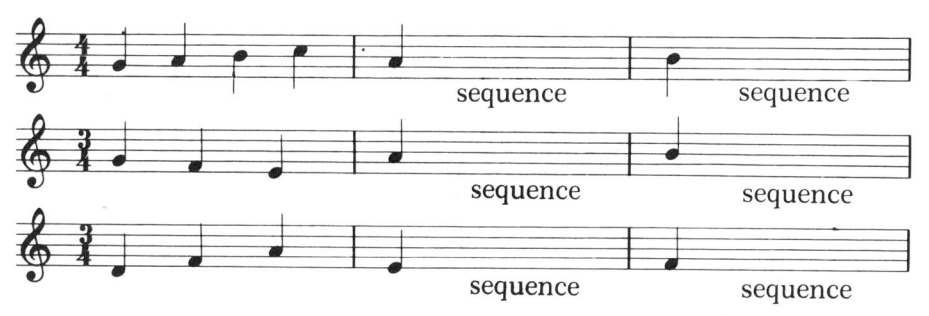

Remember that:

1. Stems on notes below the middle line go up from the right hand side of the note.
2. Stems on notes above the middle line go down from the left hand side of the note.
3. Stems on notes on the middle line can follow either rule.

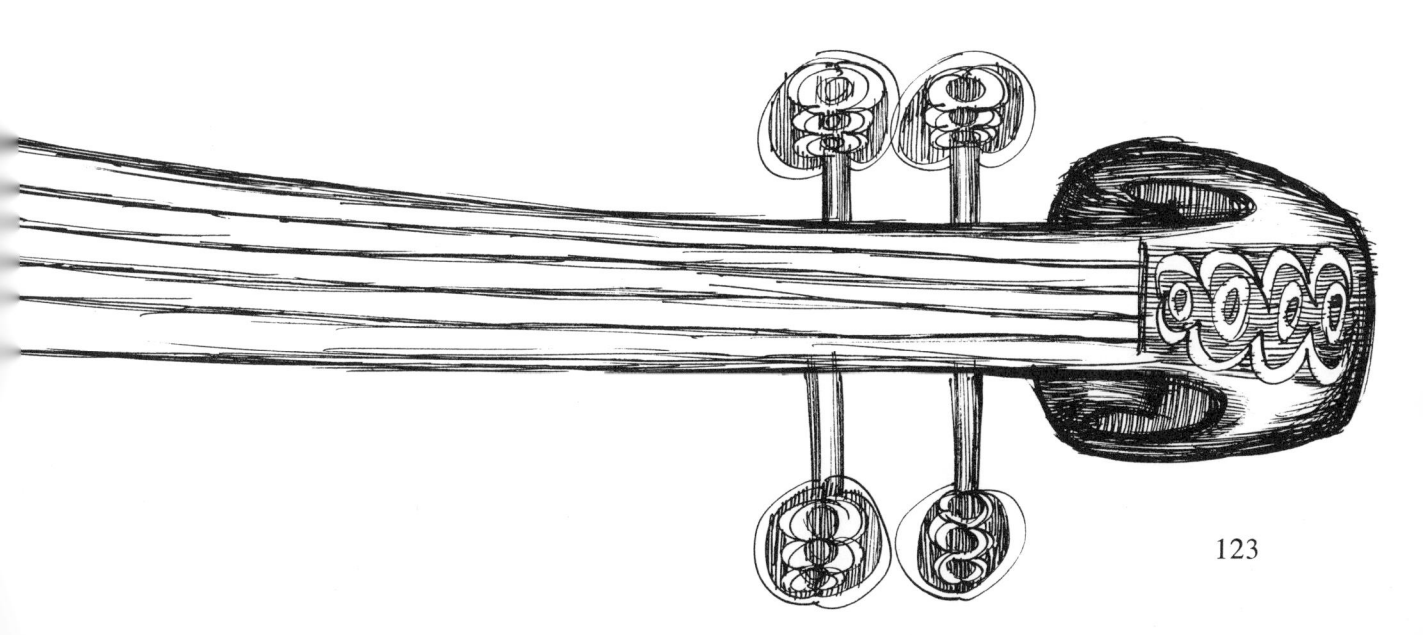

123

Aaron Copland

Aaron Copland * is a composer who was born in 1900 in Brooklyn, New York. He is still living today in the United States. Although his family owned a store and were not musicians, he became interested in music as a boy. He saved the money he earned from working in his father's store to go to France to study with the famous teacher, Nadia Boulanger ("Boo-lahn-zhay"). After coming back to the United States, he became one of America's best-known composers. His music, like most music in our day, has very strong, interesting rhythms. He also used the music of America, from folk songs and square-dance music to jazz, in his orchestral compositions.

Listen to the piece called "Hoe Down". This is a lively, noisy dance that is taken from a longer composition called "Rodeo".

Listen for:

1. The old-time fiddlers tuning up
2. The rhythm that sounds like tapping feet and clapping hands
3. The old fiddler's square dance tune
4. The use of syncopation (irregular rhythm accents).

For further listening suggestions for "Hoe Down" and more of Mr. Copland's biography, see the "Teachers Guide" to *Adventures in Music*, Grade 5, Volume 2, by Gladys and Eleanor Tipton. This piece is also recorded in *Bowmar Orchestral Library*, No. 55.

* Pronounced "Copeland".

Simple Gifts

Cheerfully

Pennsylvania Dutch Folk Song

'Tis a gift to be sim-ple, 'tis a gift to be free;

To—

This is an old folk song from Pennsylvania that is sometimes sung to the words " 'Tis a gift to be simple". Play it on your recorders. Make up your own words to complete the verse.

You can also hear this melody played on the clarinet in the seventh variation of "Appalachian Spring", by Aaron Copland.

Other Copland compositions you will enjoy are:
"Street in a Frontier Town" from "Billy the Kid Ballet Suite"; *Adventures in Music*, Grade 6, Vol. 1.
"Circus Music" from "The Red Pony"; *Adventures in Music*, Grade 3, Vol. 1.

Lullaby

Johannes Brahms

Lul - la - by and good-night, With roses be-dight,
With down o - ver - spread Is ba - by's wee bed.
Lay thee down now and rest, May thy slum - bers be blest;
Lay thee down now and rest, May thy slum - bers be blest.

What kind of tone will portray the mood of this song? Long phrases will add to the beauty of your singing. Listen to "Liebesleider Waltzes" by Brahms.

Sing Your Way Home

Smoothly

Camp Song

Sing your way home at the close of the day,

Sing your way home, drive the shad-ows a-way.

Smile all the while and wher-ev-er you roam,

You will bright-en the road, you will light-en your load,

If you sing your way home.

ABOUT THE MUSIC   You will enjoy the sound of the extra part (the small notes) in the last few bars of this piece. A small group of singers may sing it as a descant or play it on the recorders, bells, or piano.
What are the alphabetical names of the first four notes of this piece?

What are the alphabetical names of the notes in the I-chord in the key of G?
Since the first four notes are members of the G-chord, but G is not on the bottom, it is called an upside-down or *inverted* chord.

THINGS TO DO

1. Write your own tune for the four words "Sing your way home", using just the notes of the F-chord (F, A, and C in any order).
   Try what you have written on the piano.

2. Write the C-chord.
   Now write the C-chord inverted.
   Can you find more than one way of inverting the chord?

3. What patterns do you find in the last part of the music?

All Through the Night

Welsh Air

Phrase A

Sleep my child and peace at-tend thee all through the night

Phrase A

Guard-ian an-gels God will send thee all through the night

Phrase B

Soft the drow-sy hours are creep-ing, hill and vale in slum-ber steep-ing

Phrase A

I my lov-ing vig-il keep-ing all through the night.

This song has four phrases. Phrase A is repeated twice. Since the third phrase is different it is called B. This B phrase provides contrast in the song. The concluding phrase being the A phrase gives the song unity. The form of this song is AABA.

The Little Prince

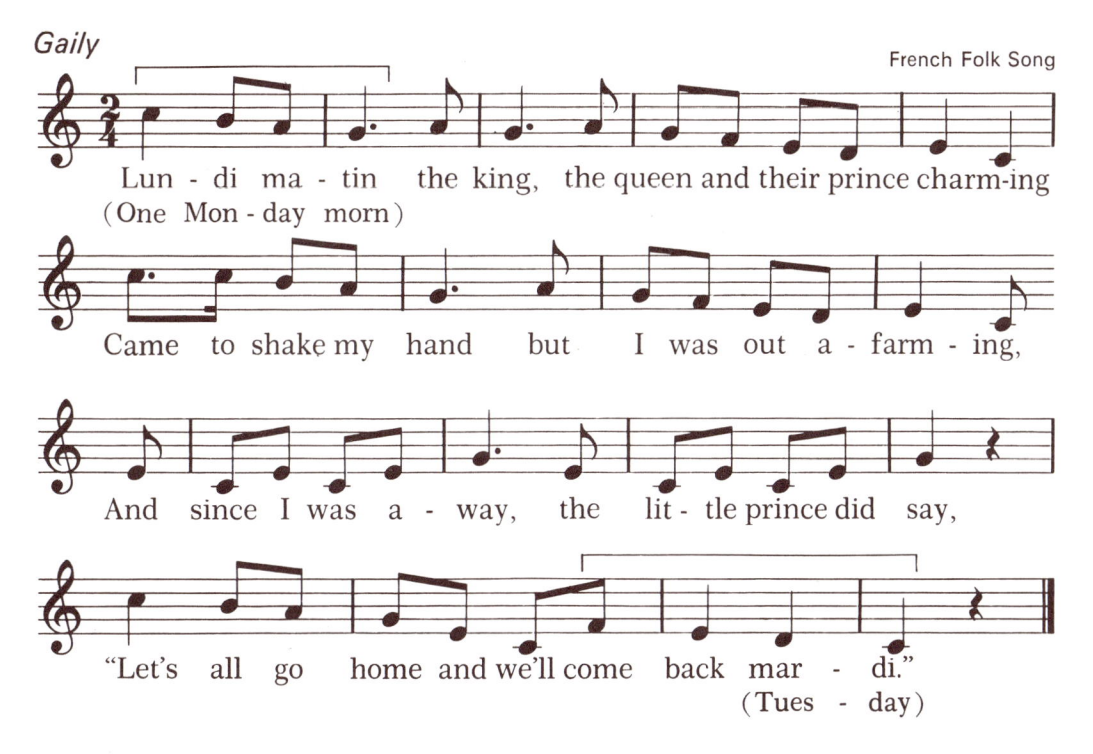

Gaily   French Folk Song

Lun - di ma - tin   the king,   the queen and their prince charm-ing
(One Mon - day morn)
Came   to shake my   hand   but   I was out a - farm - ing,
And   since I was a - way,   the lit - tle prince did say,
"Let's all go   home and we'll come back mar - di."
                                                    (Tues - day)

ABOUT THE SONG

Alan Mills, the famous Canadian folk singer, has translated this song from the French. Sing the words in English, but use the original French words for the days of the week to begin and end each verse:

lundi matin	– Monday morning	*jeudi*	– Thursday
mardi	– Tuesday	*vendredi*	– Friday
mercredi	– Wednesday	*samedi*	– Saturday
	dimanche – Sunday		

Santa Lucia

Gently swaying

Italian Folk Song

Now 'neath the sil-ver moon Ocean is glow-ing,
O'er the calm bil—-low Soft winds are blow-ing.
Here balm-y bree-zes blow, Pure joys in-vite us,
And as we gent-ly row, All things de-light us.
Hark how the sail-ors cry, Joy-ous-ly ech-oes nigh,
San—-ta— Lu— ci— -a, San-ta Lu-ci-a.
Home of fair poe-sy, Realm of pure har-mo-ny,
San—-ta— Lu— - ci— -a, San-ta Lu-ci-a.

Santa Lucia (Saint of Light) is the patron saint of fishermen.

Discover which phrases are alike.

The form is AABB.

Make your singing more expressive with long, beautiful phrases.

Juanita

Gently swaying

Spanish Song

Soft o'er the fountain Ling'ring falls the southern moon,
Far o'er the mountain Breaks the day too soon.
In thy dark eyes' splendor Where the warm light loves to dwell,
Weary looks yet tender Speak their fond farewell.
'Nita, Juanita, Ask thy soul if we should part;
'Nita, Juanita, Lean thou on my heart.

* The number 3 over the three eighth notes means that they are sung in the time usually given to two eighth notes (one beat).

Sing these two songs separately. When you are familiar with both of them, divide the class in half and have the one group sing Juanita at the same time as the other group sings Santa Lucia.
Songs that we can combine like this are called *partner songs*.
For further examples, see *Partner Songs* and *More Partner Songs*, selected and arranged by F. Beckman, and published by Ginn & Co.

Find the phrases which are similar.

Charlie Is My Darling

Scottish Folk Song

Char - lie is my dar - ling, my dar - ling, my dar - ling,
Char - lie is my dar - ling, the young ca - va - lier.

This old song was sung by the Scottish people about a famous prince, "Bonnie Prince Charlie", whom they wanted for their king.

ABOUT THE MUSIC

Although this piece is in the minor key, it should be sung briskly. Accompany the song by strumming the D minor and D7 chord simultaneously.

Oh, Dear! What Can the Matter Be?

English Folk Song

CHORUS

Oh, dear! What can the mat-ter be?

Dear, dear, what can the mat-ter be?

Oh, dear! What can the mat-ter be?

Fine

John-ny's so long at the fair.____

VERSE

1. He prom-ised to buy me a trin-ket to please me,
2. He prom-ised to bring me a bas-ket of po-sies,

And then, for a smile, Oh, he vowed he would tease me,
A gar-land of lil-ies, A gift of red ros-es,

He prom-ised to bring me a bunch of blue rib-bons
A lit-tle straw hat to set off the blue rib-bons

D.C. al Fine

To tie up my bon-ny brown hair.____
That tie up my bon-ny brown hair.____

Land of Cherry Blossoms

Chinese Melody
Arr. by Burton Kurth
Words by T. W. Woodhead

1. Here where pa-go-da bells their chimes soft-ly ring, Sweet cher-ry blos-soms blithe-ly greet the Spring; Fra-grance, beau-ty and 'witch-ing light Speak of hope and peace thro' the night.
2. Here in our age old Eas-tern land, Peace and beau-ty walk hand in hand; Fra-grant blos-soms on cher-ry bough Bring us their hope filled mes-sage now.

Note that the bareness of the accompaniment to "Land of Cherry Blossoms" helps to retain the Chinese quality of the melody.
Is this a pentatonic melody? Prove your answer. What is the form of this song?

Gin Gang Goo

Traditional

Gin - gang goo - li, goo - li, goo - li, goo - li, watch - a, gin - gang goo, gin - gang goo. Gin - gang goo - li, goo - li, goo - li, goo - li, watch - a, gin - gang goo, gin gang goo. Hey - la____, hey - la shey - la____, hey - la shey - la, hey____ la____ hoo____. Hey - la____, hey - la shey - la____, hey - la shey - la, hey - la - hoo____.

Shal - ly, wal - ly, shal - ly, wal - ly, oom - pah, oom - pah oom - pah. Gin - gang (etc.)

136

ABOUT THE MUSIC

Pronounce the *g*'s in this nonsense song as in the word "good".
Since this song requires only three chords (F, C7, and B♭ — the I, V7, and IV chords in F), it can easily be accompanied on the autoharp and/or piano.

Play two chords per bar — one on the first beat and one on the third beat.

Do you remember what the signs ‖: :‖ mean?

Fine means that the second time through, the music ends at this point.

THINGS TO DO

Turn back to page 34 and play "There's a Hole in My Bucket" in the key of G.

In your notebook:

1. Copy these phrases and put in the correct time signature at each arrow:

Boston Come-All-Ye
(*The Fishes*)

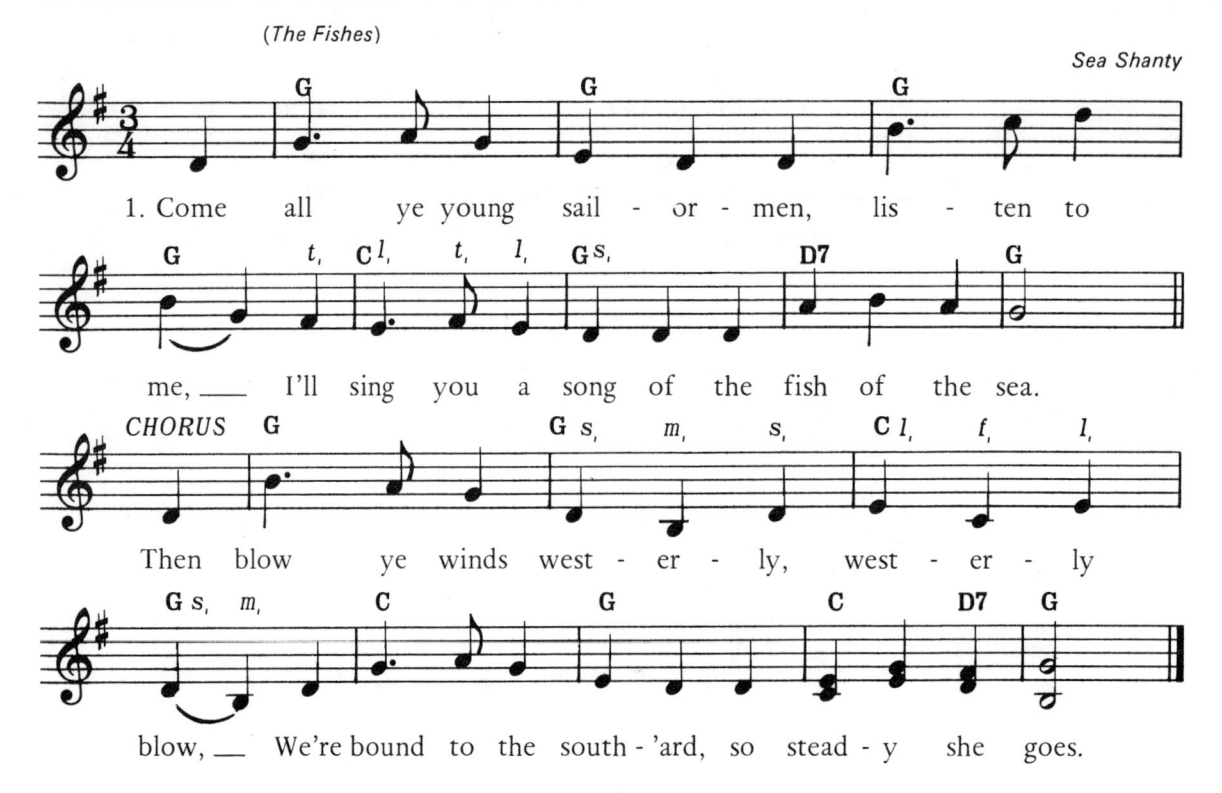

Sea Shanty

1. Come all ye young sailormen, listen to me,__ I'll sing you a song of the fish of the sea.

   CHORUS
   Then blow ye winds westerly, westerly blow,__ We're bound to the south-'ard, so steady she goes.

2. Oh, first came the whale, he's the biggest of all,
   He clumb up aloft, and let every sail fall.

3. Next came the mack'rel with his striped back,
   He hauled aft the sheets and then boarded each tack.

4. The porpoise came next with his little snout,
   He grabbed the wheel, calling, "Turn her about!"

5. Then came the minnow, the smallest of all,
   He jumped to the deck, singing "Haul, men, haul!"

6. Up jumped the tuna saying, "I am the king!
   Pull on the line, and let the bell ring."

Write a contour of the melody. Does it make you think of a stormy sea?

One of These Days
(A Round)

American Folk Song

Sing or play (on the bells or piano)

1. One of these days, Look __ up and see A wise old owl Sit-ting in a tree.
2. He'll look at you, And he'll look at me; Those two big eyes, They __ don't scare me.
3. One of these nights When __ rain-drops fall, He'll give a hoot, He'll __ give a call.

1. One of these days, Look __ up and see A wise old owl Sit-ting in a tree.
2. He'll look at you, And he'll look at me; Those two big eyes, They __ don't scare me.
3. One of these nights When __ rain-drops fall, He'll give a hoot, He'll __ give a call.

This song is a round. The part each group sings is on a separate staff. Group 1 sings the first, third, and fifth lines. Group 2 sings the second, fourth, and sixth lines. Listen to the other part.

Follow On!

(Echo Song)

Old Song

Come a-long, Sing a song, Follow me; It is eas-y as you see. Ev-'ry day, In this way Just re-peat Till the tune's com-plete.

Come a-long, Sing a song, Fol-low me; It is eas-y, as you see. Ev-'ry day, In this way Just re-peat, Till the tune's com-plete.

Girl's Dance Song

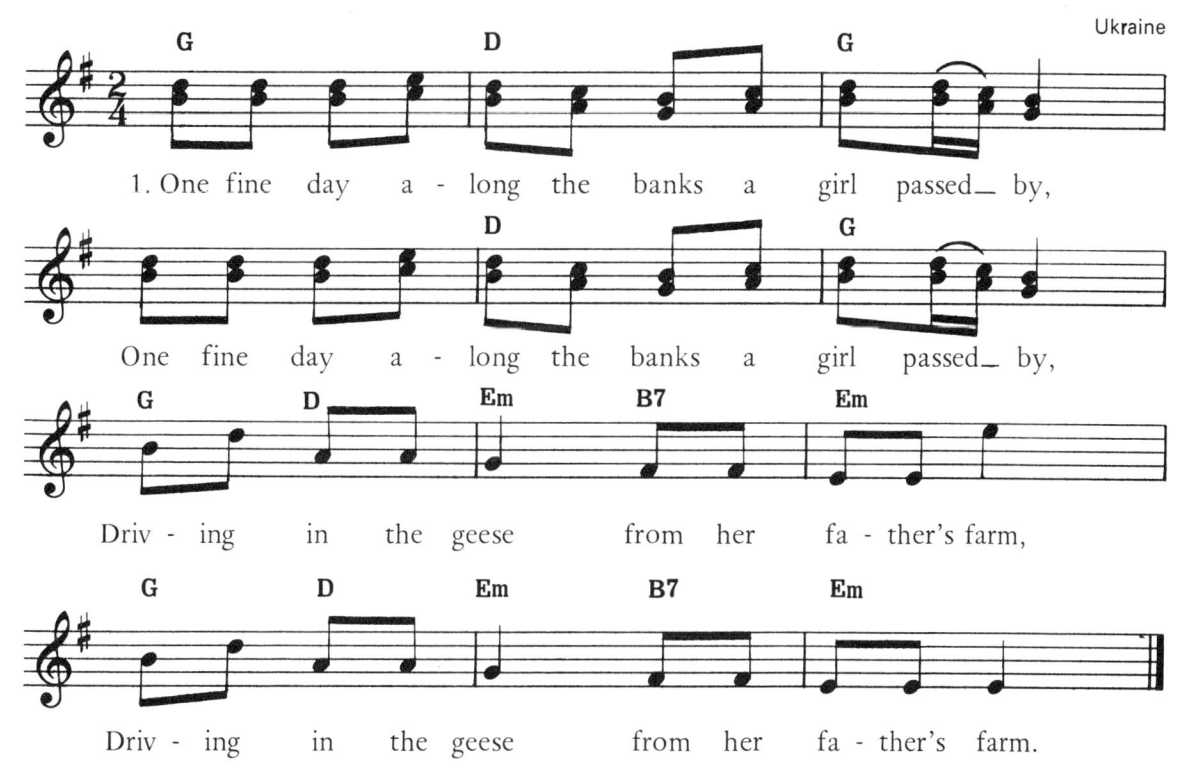

Ukraine

1. One fine day a-long the banks a girl passed by,
   One fine day a-long the banks a girl passed by,
   Driv-ing in the geese from her fa-ther's farm,
   Driv-ing in the geese from her fa-ther's farm.

Copyright 1956, by Novello & Company Limited

2. Come along, you foolish geese, come follow me,
   If I sell you surely 'twill do no harm.

3. So she took the geese and sold them every one.
   Sought some brief delight till the day was done.

4. So she hired a bagpiper for the day:
   Play, good piper, drive all my cares away.

5. O good piper, play, and play again,
   I would fain forget all my grief and pain.

E. V. de B.

Discover phrases which are repeated. Find the octave jump.
Suggest instrumental accompaniment.

Tzena

Israeli Folk Song

Tze - na, tze - na, tze - na, tze - na,

Can't you hear the mu - sic play - ing

In ____ the cit - y square?
I'll ____ be danc - ing there.

Tze - na, tze - na, join the cel - e - bra - tion,

There'll be peo-ple there from ev - 'ry na - tion!

Dawn will find us laugh-ing in the sun - light,

There'll ____ be danc - ing there!

After you know this song well, with everyone singing in unison, you may sing it as a round. The second part begins as the first group sings "Tzena" (tsay-nuh) for the second section.

The Papaya Tree

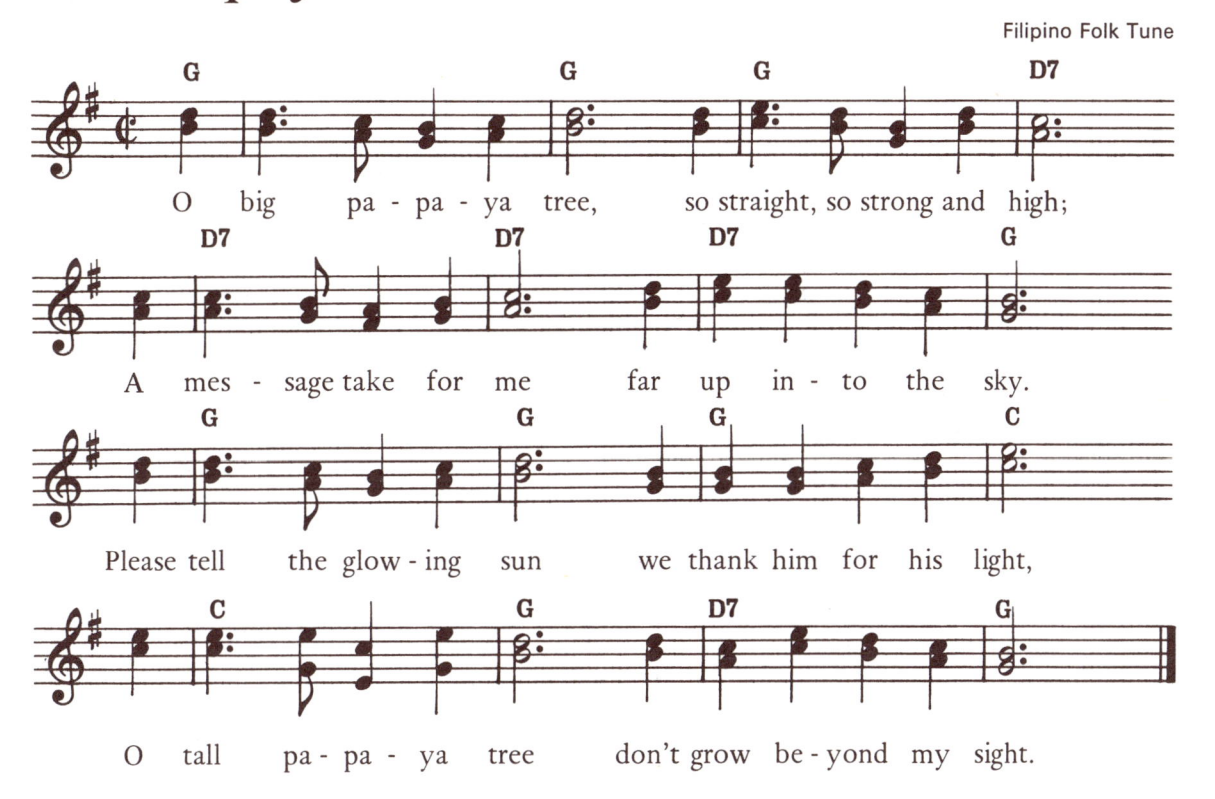

Filipino Folk Tune

O big papaya tree, so straight, so strong and high;
A message take for me far up into the sky.
Please tell the glowing sun we thank him for his light,
O tall papaya tree don't grow beyond my sight.

The second part may be sung or played on the bells.

143

Will Ye No Come Back Again?

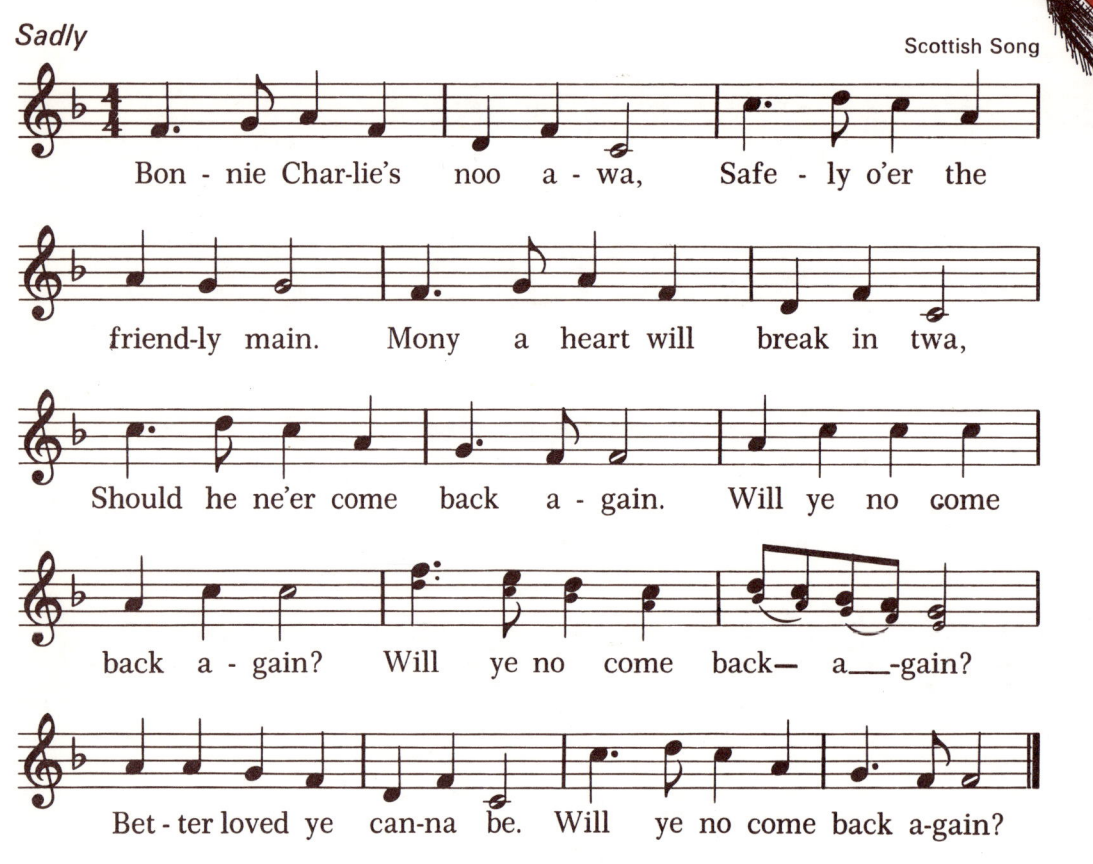

Sadly

Scottish Song

Bon-nie Char-lie's noo a-wa, Safe-ly o'er the friend-ly main. Mony a heart will break in twa, Should he ne'er come back a-gain. Will ye no come back a-gain? Will ye no come back—a-gain? Bet-ter loved ye can-na be. Will ye no come back a-gain?

The words in Scottish dialect mean the following:

noo	– now		*twa*	– two
awa	– away		*ye*	– you
main	– sea		*no*	– not
mony	– many		*canna*	– cannot

REVIEW 4

1. Write the correct word in your notebook:
   (a) A song with an A B pattern is said to be in ....
   (b) Two notes with the same name and separated by eight notes are an .... apart.
   (c) The bass viol is a .... instrument.
   (d) The note below the key note is called the ....

   leading note
   two part form
   octave
   string

2. Sing these phrases after the first note has been played on bells, pitch-pipe, or piano:

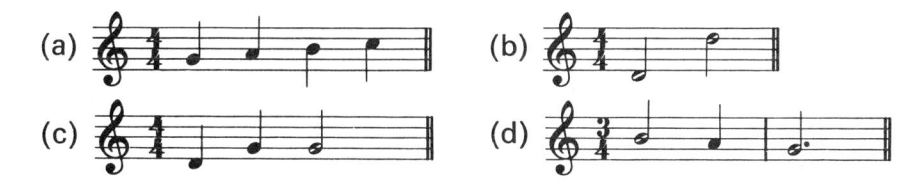

   (a) (b)
   (c) (d)

3. Write notes an octave above each of these notes:

4. In your notebook, fill in each bar with the correct number of quarter notes. ♩

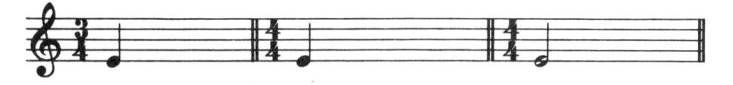

5. In your notebook, write the tonic sol-fa symbols for the notes in (a) and (b) below.

   (a)
   (b)

6. In your notebook, write the time names for the notes in the following passage.

FINGERING CHART FOR THE RECORDER

○ Open hole   ● Closed hole   ◐ Partly closed hole

[Fingering chart showing notes from C to G with corresponding finger positions for thumb, left hand (1st, 2nd, 3rd finger), and right hand (1st, 2nd, 3rd, 4th finger)]

1 = German fingering   2 = Baroque fingering

Glossary of Musical Terms and Signs

ACCENT: > this sign indicates a special emphasis or stress to be put on a particular note or beat.

BAR LINE: a vertical line to divide the music into measures, sometimes called bars.

BAR: (also called a measure) is the music in the space between two bar lines.

CHORD: three or more tones sounded at the same time.

CRESCENDO: < *gradual* increase in loudness of tone.

DECRESCENDO: > *gradual* decrease in loudness of tone.

DESCANT: a counter or independent melody usually sung by a few voices above the main melody.

FERMATA: ⌢ or ⌣ indicates that a note is to be held longer than full value.

FLAT: (♭) a symbol or sign that lowers the pitch of a tone by one half step.

HALF STEP: the shortest distance between two notes. The half steps occur between the third and fourth (m-f) and seventh and eighth (t-d) degrees of the scale.

INTERVAL: the distance in pitch from one note to another, counting from the bottom note. For example:

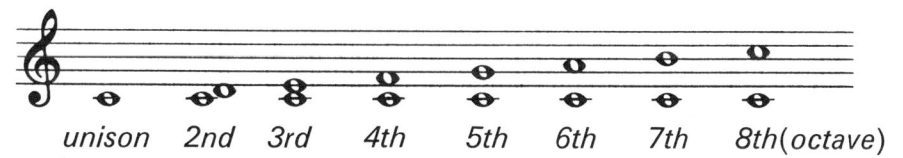

unison   2nd   3rd   4th   5th   6th   7th   8th (octave)

KEY SIGNATURE: sharps or flats placed on the staff at the beginning of a composition to indicate the key.

MAJOR SCALE: a series of eight tones in a definite pattern of whole and half steps.

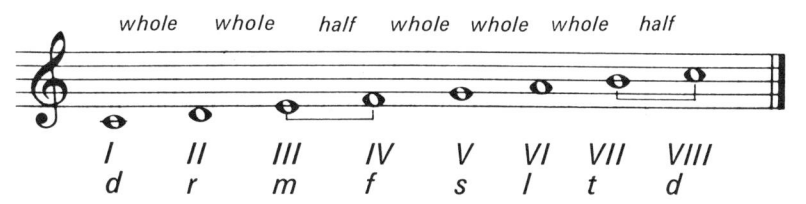

whole whole half whole whole whole half

I   II   III   IV   V   VI   VII   VIII
d   r   m   f   s   l   t   d

METRE SIGNATURE: Examples: $\frac{2}{4}$; $\frac{3}{4}$; $\frac{4}{4}$; $\frac{6}{8}$;

The top numeral tells the number of beats within a bar (measure). The lower figure tells the kind of note which receives one beat or count.

MINOR SCALE: a series of eight notes in a definite pattern.

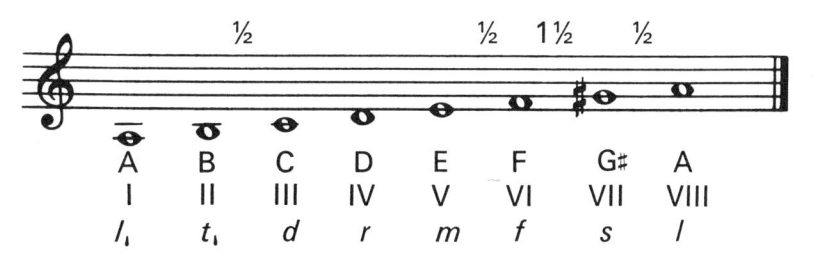

½   ½   1½   ½

A   B   C   D   E   F   G♯   A
I   II III IV V   VI VII VIII
l, t, d   r   m   f   s   l

NATURAL SIGN: (♮) this sign appears immediately in front of a note to cancel, for one measure, a sharp or flat which was previously indicated in the key signature or by an accidental.

147

NOTES:	signs or symbols designed to tell how long to sing or play a note. For example, ○ whole note 𝅗𝅥. dotted half note 𝅗𝅥 half note ♩ quarter note ♪ eighth note ♪ sixteenth note, usually appears ♫♫ or ♬
PENTATONIC SCALE:	a five-tone scale which does not use the fourth (fah) and seventh (te) degrees of the scale. The five black keys of the piano fit this scale. In tonic sol-fa syllables the scale looks like this: l, d r m s l.
PERCUSSION INSTRUMENTS:	instruments played by striking or shaking. For example: drum, rhythm sticks, tambourine, gourds, etc.
REPEAT SIGNS:	(:‖) signs which tell us which section of the music is to be repeated.
RESTS:	signs that measure silence between notes or phrases. ▬ whole rest 𝄾 eighth rest ▬ half rest 𝄿 sixteenth rest 𝄽 quarter rest
ROOT:	the tone on which a chord is built. It is sometimes called I or doh.
SHARP:	♯ a sign that raises the pitch of a tone by one half step.
SLUR:	a curved line placed above or below two or more notes of different pitch which indicates that these notes are to be sung on one word or syllable.
STAFF:	The five horizontal lines and four spaces upon which notes and other musical symbols are placed.
SYNCOPATION:	an unexpected or misplaced strong accent on a weak beat. For examples, see "Canoe Song", "New River Train", "Mañana".
TIED NOTES:	two notes of the same pitch connected by a curved line. The notes are held for the value of both notes.
TREBLE CLEF:	(the G clef because it circles the second line of the staff) this sign 𝄞 determines the names for the lines and spaces of the staff.

Index

A la Claire Fontaine, 103
Accidentals, 43
Ach Ja!, 80
Ah! Poor Bird, 77
Ah! Si Mon Moine Voulait Danser, 52
All People that on Earth do Dwell, 3
All Through the Night, 128
Amsterdam, 40
Auld Lang Syne, 96
Autoharp accompaniments, 26, 36, 40, 42, 48, 50, 58, 59, 62, 63, 64, 66, 70, 71, 73, 74, 78, 80, 82, 84, 88, 97, 103, 113, 116, 120, 130, 136, 138, 141, 142, 143

Bell Doth Toll, The, 25
Beside Thy Cradle Here I Stand, 56
Blank notation, 67
Bonavist' Harbour, 55
Bonhomme! Bonhomme!, 122
Boston Come-All-Ye, 138
Brother Come and Dance, 30

Canoe Song, 68
Can't You Dance the Polka?, 120
Charlie Is My Darling, 132
Chords (see also Harmony)
  C7-chord, 73
  D-chord, 77
  D minor chord, 77
  F-chord, 73
  F minor chord, 90
  V7-chord, 67
  inverted, 127
  I-chord, 11, 47
Christmas carols, 56-62
Christmas Is Here, 61
Come Let's Dance, 65
Copland, Aaron, 124
Cornish May Song, 110
Cricket Takes a Wife, The, 74
Curwen, 1
Czech Dance, 91

Dance Carol, 58
Dance songs, 4, 18, 30, 42, 50, 80
Dashing Away with the Smoothing Iron, 48

Deaf Woman's Courtship, The, 6
Deck the Halls, 57
Descant, 64, 69, 71, 85, 127
Dialogue songs, 6, 20, 22, 34, 44, 46, 78
Doon The Moor, 121
Drums and Tambourines, 82
Dynamics, 18-9, 65

Easter Hymn, 108
Echo Carol, 60
Echo songs, 36, 60, 140
En Roulant, Ma Boule, 116
Eskimo Lullaby, An, 72

Fingering Chart for the Recorder, 146
Fire's Burning, 10
Fishes, The, 138
Follow On!, 140
For Health and Strength, 11
Form, 82, 85, 128, 130
French words, songs with, 52, 83, 103, 116, 122
Frère Jacques, 83
Fum Fum Fum, 59

Gin Gang Goo, 136
Girl's Dance Song, 141
Greedy Girl, The, 66
Green Dress, The, 18
Grieg, Edvard, 100

Hallowe'en, 28
Hand signs, 1
  songs with, 3, 4, 5, 6, 8, 18
Hannukkah song, 63
Harmony, 94
Haru Ga Kita, 113
Heigh Ho, Anybody Home?, 90

Ifca's Castle, 76
Intervals, 53, 83

Juanita, 131

King Arthur, 20
Kookaburra, 97

149

Land of Cherry Blossoms, 134
Land of the Silver Birch, 114
Leading note, 82
Little Night Music, A, 38
Little Prince, The, 129
Lukey's Boat, 5
Lullaby (Brahms), 126

Mañana, 71
Melody, 32
Michael Finnigin, 64
Moldau, The, 79
Mozart, 38-41
My Candles, 63
My Goose, 11
My Hat It Has Three Corners, 73
My Homeland, 101

New River Train, 70
Night Herding Song, 104
Now Thank We All Our God, 16

Octave, 102
Oh, Dear! What Can the Matter Be?, 133
O How Lovely Is The Evening, 98
Old Joe Clarke, 42
Old Texas, 36
Old Woman and the Pedlar, The, 24
Oliver Cromwell, 46
On The Moor, 109
One of These Days, 139

Papaya Tree, The, 143
Partner songs, 130-1
Patapan, 62
Peer Gynt Suite Theme, 101
Pentatonic scale, 35
Pentatonic songs, 34, 36, 68, 96, 114, 144

Recorder, playing the, 92-3, 98-9, 101, 117, 146
Reviews, 54, 86, 111, 145
Rhythm, 4, 7, 41, 47, 49, 51, 53, 69, 72, 81
Rhythm drills, 11, 12, 20, 22, 23
Rhythm round, 7
Rhythm syllables, 9

Rig-a-Jig-Jig, 50
Rounds, 10, 11, 12, 23, 25, 65, 68, 77, 83, 90, 97, 98, 109, 139

Santa Lucia, 130
Scales
  A major, 58
  A minor, 59
  A flat, 87
  D minor, 77
  E flat, 51
  E minor, 68
  F minor, 90
  G minor, 62
  harmonic minor, 77
  major (C, F, G, D), 31
  pentatonic, 35
Schubert, 89
Sequences, 119
'Simmons, 4
Simple Gifts, 125
Sing Your Way Home, 127
Slumber Song, 89
Snoring Man, The, 118
Some Folks Do, 22
Spring Has Come, 113
Spring Round, 109
Streets of Laredo, 84
Sweet Nightingale, 88
Syncopation, 69, 70, 71

There's a Hole in My Bucket, 34
Time names, 9, 13, 19
songs with, 10, 11, 12, 20, 23
Tonic sol-fa syllables, 1
Tzena, 142

Violin, 38-9
Voyageur Song, 87

Way Up on The Mountain, 102
We Are Musicians, 27
Weggis, 15
We're on the Upward Trail, 12
Where Is John?, 23
Who Did Swallow Jonah?, 44
Who Has Seen The Wind?, 112
Will Ye No Come Back Again?, 144
Wishing Well, The, 8
Wraggle-Taggle Gypsies, O!, 78

150